Hanging Around Musicians

Gareth Ashton

EMPIRE
PUBLICATIONS

First published in 2014

EMPIRE PUBLICATIONS
1 Newton Street, Manchester M1 1HW
© Gareth Ashton 2014

ISBN 978-1-909360-25-9

Printed and bound by CPI Group (UK) Ltd, Croydon, CR0 4YY.

Contents

ACKNOWLEDGEMENTS

Special thanks go out to the following for their assistance in allowing me to break into their memory banks and plunder what they had accumulated over the years. I have made every effort to clarify events into a truthful conclusion;

Steve Bainbridge, Phillip Charles Baker, David Barnett, Tony Beesley, Bob Booth, Karen Booth, Mark Broxup, Carl Fisher, Steven Hall, Jock Hart, John 'Segs' Jennings, Dale Jowett, Howie Kanes, Johnny Keep, Alan Longden, Stephen Longden, Manchester District Music Archive, Steve Mardy, Dennis Matthews, Neil Mclennan, Thomas Mensforth, Steve Morris, Andy Mottram, Gary Perkins, Dave Ruffy, Andy Salvin, Paul Scott, Starch E. Smith, Bill Sykes and Martin Toner@SK23 Design.

"The music business is a cruel and shallow money trench, a long plastic hallway where thieves and pimps run free, and good men die like dogs. There's also a negative side."

HUNTER S. THOMSON

The 'Music business', 'Show business', fame and the leisure industry are all fickle and certainly far from "fair". The business of music however. can be an uplifting, mood changing even life-changing thing.

Q. "What do you call someone who hangs around musicians?"

A. "A drummer"

For me drumming has been a way out of the ghetto I was living in as a teenager and I've been lucky enough to make living from music since 1977. Lucky me!

I first met Gareth in 1980 we were both supporting punk rock meisters/jokers "the Damned", he with the Irritators, me with the Ruts.

I have met him a few times since and have found him to be a sharply dressed chap, a keen timekeeper both quick witted and affable!

Last year in 2013 we met in Scotland and I was pleased to hear he was writing this book 'Hanging around Musicians'

Having read his tales and anecdotes, I am most impressed, here is one man's account of the peaks and troughs of a musical career,

Gareth is a fine raconteur and it is as honest and funny a read as I've had in a long while.

David Ruffy

INTRODUCTION

1977: Year zero? This was the year that would shape the rest of my life. Was I being non-conformist? Bloody minded? A personal crusade against what you were expected to be? Not really. Today it might be classed as a career move, or attention seeking. I'd class it as a natural progression. punk music was for my youth just like every other musical genre before it and since. We weren't pioneers, because the teds, and the mods and rockers, skinheads, suedeheads, hippies, even the glam rockers all had a part to play in fusing punk music together. But it was our turn now, so just leave us alone to do what we want to do like they did in their time. But of course they didn't. We threatened them. Which was weird because I hated violence; visual confrontation rather than physical confrontation was my weapon of choice. You must understand that at that time our numbers were very few, but the newspapers had painted a warped picture of vomit and safety pins. We were the future; your future.

Officially, punk in its original guise was dead by 1977. Record companies had cottoned onto the fact that there was money to be made from this new movement, following their initial fear that they would be taken for mugs as the Sex Pistols had so expertly achieved. All the front runners had secured deals with the major labels, and the good, the bad, and the mediocre had their shot at fame too, which was great because all of a sudden Top of the Pops became more exciting to watch. Amongst all the dross of the chart pop, you'd get The Adverts, The Jam, Buzzcocks, and the Sex Pistols (eventually). The Clash refused to go on the programme but there were enough new bands coming through to enrich our Thursday night viewing. I can still hear my Dad moaning and tutting at the 'scruffy sods' on the screen, which was how it should be. If your parents like the same music as you, you're doing something wrong. Or perhaps they are!

maxell UR
POSITION
IEC TYPE I · NORMAL

UR | maxell

A DATE ___ Pre-Punk
N.R. ___ 1963 ○YES ○NO

The Faces - Stay With Me
The Beatles - Rain
Thunderclap Newman
    — Something In the Air
T-Rex - Metal Guru
Ike + Tina - Fingerpoppin'
The Temptations - Cloud 9
Small Faces - Tin Soldier
Little Richard - Lucille

B DATE ___ Pre-Punk ○YES ○NO
N.R. ___ 1977

Mary Love - Lay His Burden
The Stooges - Wannabe
    your Dog
Curtis Mayfield - Move On Up
Slade - C'mon Feel the Noise
David Bowie - Warszawa
Funkadelic - Cosmic Slop
Dusty Springfield
    — Goin' Back

1. Apathy's A Drag

The '70's didn't really have a lot going for it. A lot of the monochrome archive film footage from the era shows political unrest; football hooliganism; mass unemployment; 3 day weeks; television programmes cancelled due to yet another strike orchestrated by electricians, or a dispute over the length of tea break at the car manufacturing plant. Rubbish bags piled high in the streets, rat infested tower block estates, set against a backdrop of a grey, grim, joyless landscape. On the down side though was the music. With a few exceptions such as Bowie, Bolan, Slade, Roxy Music, the music industry was awash with sterile groups. Some of whom were constructed by record producers using session musicians to play, and sometimes sing the tunes, which were then fronted by a pretty face to sell sugary songs with meaningless lyrics, miming on Top of the Pops. The same show that in 1964 had set out to reflect the bourgeoning, vibrant youth culture of the day had ended up in 1976 as an embarrassing low brow variety show, although in its defence it was only reflecting the paltry choices on offer at the time.

Britain was going through a very low point musically but there were the odd chinks of light emerging with bands like Dr.Feelgood, Kilburn and the High Roads featuring Ian Dury, The 101'ers – who were a stepping stone to greater things for John Mellor, subsequently renaming himself as Joe Strummer, and Brinsley Schwartz which included Nick Lowe, the man who would go on to produce the first official punk single. These bands and many more like them were trying to mix it up with their high energy, fast delivery of a mixture of cover versions as well as their own material. They later became pigeon-holed (rather lazily in my opinion) as 'Pub Rock', because that's where these groups mainly plied their trade.

This was a back to basics approach to music that would pave the way for punk and there were a few bands who decided to play that bit harder and louder to inevitably become associated with the fledgling scene. But on the opposite side of the coin were the bands that were too big to go on Top of the Pops, sending the newish medium of a promotional videotape instead. They didn't want to get too close to their audience. Playing football stadiums or Greek amphitheatres, the likes of Pink Floyd and Led Zeppelin had lost touch with reality (if they ever had it) and the self-gratifying, parasitical record companies were raking in the cash. Rod Stewart had gone from the no nonsense, gritty rock of The Faces to the turgid 'Sailing', chasing the Yankee dollar. The industry needed a kick up the arse. punk gave the music back to the audience not only through the lyrical content but also because they were able to touch the band due to the small venues and sometimes lack of stage.

Unfortunately I write this through the benefit of hindsight. The year that punk broke didn't include me. The Peak District town where I lived in 1976 was a million miles away from the turbulent and unruly goings on in London, a scene perpetuated by a small, like-minded group of people, who initially were non musicians, but collectively shared a common goal which embodied itself in an insubordinate attitude towards the machinations of an out of touch music industry. It would take about 12 months before the epiphany of punk manifested itself with me.

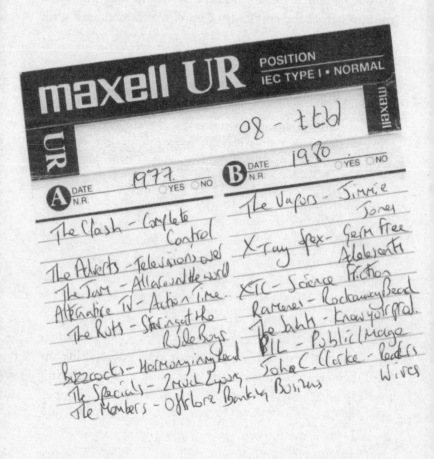

maxell **UR** POSITION IEC TYPE I • NORMAL

1977 - 80

A DATE 1977 N.R. ○ YES ○ NO

B DATE 1980 N.R. ○ YES ○ NO

The Clash - Complete Control

The Adverts - Televisions over

The Jam - All around the world

Alternative TV - Action Time

The Ruts - Staring at the Rude Boys

Buzzcocks - Harmony in my head

The Specials - 2 Much 2 young

The Members - Offshore Banking Business

The Vapors - Jimmie Jones

X-Ray Spex - Germ Free Adolescents

XTC - Science Fiction

Ramones - Rockaway Beach

The Jah - Know your rights

PIL - Public Image

John C. Clarke - Beasley

Wives

2. Looking For New

WEDNESDAY 24TH AUGUST 1977

This was the day that changed everything. Elvis Presley and Groucho Marx had died within a week of each other earlier in the month. The National Front was trying to spread their vitriolic doctrine amongst the ignorant and impressionable youth of the inner cities and beyond, causing unrest and mistrust between the black and white communities, plus the Police seemed to have their own agenda with a stop and search policy primarily targeted on the dark side of the street. Up here in the hills of Derbyshire these events may as well have been happening on Mars. There was no social media or rolling news then, your only outlet for information was at 6, 9, or 10 o'clock which was read to you in an anodyne accent. I was 13 years old and life up until that time meant spending every waking hour playing football until it went dark, or riding my Blue Chopper bike up and down the road of our council estate in Chapel en-le-Frith, a small town whose only contribution to this septic isle was the Ferodo brake lining factory, where my father, and what seemed like the rest of the surrounding population at that time, worked.

I tended to make my own entertainment due to the fact that I was the last of 4 children, with 7 years between me and the next eldest. I have 1 sister, Julie and 2 brothers, Kevin and Andrew. This Wednesday in August would mark an epoch in the way my life would evolve, because it was the day of the first showing of a new programme on Granada TV called simply, 'Marc'. One of the few current musical interests I had at that time was Marc Bolan, who, tragically, would be dead within a months' time, aged just 29 years old. He had just been given his own show in which he featured the pop stars of the day, such as Bay City Rollers and Showaddywaddy, but to his credit he also used the programme to promote and give air time to up and coming bands and musicians. This was the first in the series and after the credits had rolled and Marc had finished his first (mimed) song, he breathlessly introduced his first act on his first show; The Jam.

Bang! The first thing that struck me was the attitude of the singer, and then realising that there were only three of them, but the noise they made was so energetic and full on that it made me sit up and listen. They were singing about 'looking for new' and wanting a 'reaction' and asking for a 'youth explosion' and the music reflected this perfectly. But what really impressed me the most and what made them so special, is that towards the end of the song the drummer dropped his sticks and the last few bars of the song ended in chaos with the singer giving him a look of utter disdain and irritation. The fact that something had gone wrong, instead of being played faultlessly and soullessly only enhanced their appeal and got me thinking, I could do that! It was a source of deep regret that I had succeeded in missing the first 12 months of the punk era, arguably it's most important and some would say unadulterated period, before the sound of bandwagons being not only jumped on, but feverously plundered of every last nut and bolt until the wheels fell off. But this was of no consequence to me;

it was time to dig the new breed. I needed to join a band. How difficult could that be?

3. COME BACK WHEN YOU'VE LEARNT TO PLAY.

Music ran in the family as my father was a drummer for various show bands in the fifties and sixties and I grew up watching him play at the Buxton Working Men's Club in the early 70's. My older brother Kevin had been in bands in the local area, starting off on drums, then played both bass and lead guitar. My Mum and I went to see him once at what was then the local picture house in Buxton. I don't know if it was something that I instigated or not, it just seems funny why my mother would want to sit through what was very loud, very heavy rock music, surrounded by bearded blokes and their lank-haired girlfriends who smelt as though they had bathed in the acrid scent that was Petula Oil.

There was always music around the house whether it was my parents' Perry Como and Jim Reeves albums or my brothers' and sisters' choices. Sometimes even now when a certain record comes on the radio it takes me back. It's difficult to describe the way I feel when I hear songs like Thunderclap Newman's 'Something in the Air', still one of my favourite tunes. It transports me back to 1969 and I can visualise the music but not a specific memory or occasion, it's just a collage of sound coupled with a sense of déjà vu.

My musical experiences prior to seeing The Jam were restricted to an encyclopaedic knowledge of The Beatles, a penchant for T-Rex's The Slider album, and an alleged fondness for dancing around the living room to my sister's copy of The Small Faces first album. Although I only have her word for this, it would explain the massive influence that Kenney Jones would have on my style of playing. I absolutely adored The Small Faces but the record had a big chunk missing like someone had taken a bite out of it, which was a shame because it meant that I never heard 'Sorry She's Mine' all the way through until my teens. All the big bands played at The Pavilion Gardens in Buxton, a fate that I have achieved many times since. I went to a Beatles convention about 20 years ago and a guy who claimed to be the original Father Mackenzie from the song 'Eleanor Rigby' had a photocopied picture of The Fab Four in the very dressing room that the band that I was in at the time had been photographed in. He told me that it was his only copy, but after much begging and pleading I asked him that if I sent him some money would he get me a copy of it and send it to me. Two weeks later it appeared in the post and he had signed it! There is a statue in The Cavern Walks shopping arcade in Liverpool dedicated to him, a proper gentleman.

As I got older the influence of my father started to lean me towards putting my efforts into learning to play like him. I didn't have a drum kit so I improvised by arranging cushions on the family sofa. Using the left hand seated part for the snare drum, 2 cushions above, one left one right for the rack toms, and the right hand seated part as a floor tom, the left hand arm was the hi-hat and the right hand arm was the ride cymbal, armed with a pair of my mother's finest knitting needles for sticks, away I went drumming along to The Beatles complete catalogue playing on the record player (anyone under the age of 18 ask your parents for an explanation what a record player is and watch them get dewy eyed and rant on about how soulless and mechanical this downloading thing is nowadays, and there was nothing like going out buying a 'single' or 'L.P.' and spending hours looking at it before finally waiting your turn on the stereo system to play it). Ringo Starr was a great teacher, despite acquiring a (misguided) reputation for not being a particularly proficient drummer; just listen to Rain, She Said She Said, and Strawberry Fields Forever. He was perfect for learning to as the most important thing for a drummer in my opinion is keeping time. That might seem like a ridiculous thing to say but the amount of drummers I have seen who speed up and slowdown is frightening. As brilliant and unique as he was - could you imagine trying to emulate Keith Moon when half the time even he didn't know what he was doing? For instance, if you were starting to learn the piano, you wouldn't go straight to Chopin's Piano Concerto No.1 would you? You would start with something like 'Three Blind Mice' perhaps, because you start with the rudiments and work your way up.

Slowly but surely I progressed onto playing along to 10cc's Live And Let Live album, moving on from the cushions to sitting on a chair behind an imaginary drum kit but still retaining the services of a pair of No. 9 knitting needles. I had the configuration of the kit in my minds' eye. The songs up until then that I was copying were slow to mid tempo, which was ideal to get my technique and co-ordination honed and stood me in good stead when things were to get a lot faster. Playing at high speed and remaining tight was quite a difficult skill to perfect but that's what practise makes. There would be other improvisations along the way, including an afternoon spent at Carl Fisher's house down the road, using his mother's best pans, Tupperware tubs, wooden spoons and any other random kitchen utensils that sprung to hand. Carl later went on to front Blitz, one of the leading protagonists of the Oi! movement at the start of the eighties. We were playing along to all sorts of stuff, from Bowie's 'Low' album, which I absolutely loved and which led me on a tangent to other 'filmic' types of artists like Brian Eno and David Byrne, Can and later The Blue Nile and David Sylvian's solo material. We both shared a love of The Beatles and I used to lend Carl my brothers' albums. Abbey Road was, and remains, his favourite.

His first album purchase was the 'Rock 'n' Roll Music' compilation, which had some lesser well known Beatles recordings, such as 'Matchbox' and 'Bad Boy'. At that time The Beatles had all their singles re-released in a boxed set which meant that they were re-entering the charts. Also, Rock and Roll music was experiencing a resurgence thanks to the pub rock scene and a revival in general throughout the country. Although we would never have admitted it at the time, that music was very similar to punk with its raw, stripped down sound. I saw punk as a backlash to it because it was dwelling in the past and we were all about creating something in the present for the future. Carl would also go on about a band whose single he had bought and was very insistent that I listen to it, so he brought it up to my house and I sat there and dutifully listened to it as we sat on the bed. The A side I wasn't too keen on but the B side was much better I thought, and giving it my best Juke Box Jury opinion, my first impression was that it sounded like Status Quo and was not as rowdy as the A side. That was my official assessment of God Save the Queen c/w Did You No Wrong by The Sex Pistols, but opinions are like arseholes; everyone's got one.

After my epiphany of seeing The Jam performing 'All Around The World' I went up to Buxton with Carl to buy the record. I called round at his house, and was greeted at the door with him stood in front of me with a bright yellow mohair jumper, a la Captain Sensible, which made me feel very square and dull dressed in my snorkel parka, jeans and boots. The looks he got on the bus were priceless. This was the first time that many of them would have seen a 'punk rocker' in the flesh, having only read about them in the newspapers and seen them on television. For the record (no pun intended) he purchased Pretty Vacant. Carl was, and still is, a highly intelligent, and passionate person who taught me a lot about just being yourself and not worrying what other people thought about you.

4. WE'RE A GARAGE BAND.

THE RUIN. 1979-1980.

TIM IRRGANG – VOCALS.

STEVE BAINBRIDGE – GUITAR.

DAVE BARNETT – BASS.

JOHN GODDARD – BASS.

GARETH ASHTON – DRUMS.

The punk scene was full of pseudonyms such as Sid Vicious, Johnny Rotten, Joe Strummer and T.V. Smith to name a few, and we were quick to add to that illustrious list. I was Mal Nutrition on account of my 7 stone muscle free body, and John Goddard was Johnny Wobb on bass guitar in tribute to Jah Wobble, the bassist in Public Image Limited. John once arrived at school with a dead bird safety pinned to his school blazer. Very decadent! On guitar was Steve 'Bumbridge' Bainbridge, Tim 'Von' Irrgang was the singer and was of German descent, and therefore we had a European flavour to our ranks. Dave Barnett, or Percy Cution as he named himself, was on bass as well (not sure how we ended up with 2 bassists) and was unfortunately on the receiving end of some pretty harsh treatment which still fills me with guilt to this day. He was sacked on at least two occasions for his sub-standard playing, which was quite ironic because John was no better, but was kept in the band probably because he was better looking and attracted a higher proportion of female audience members. Quite how it ended up with the 5 of us is also sketchy, but I remember there were a few people in the running for lead vocals, bass, and lead guitar. The idea to start the group was born on a school field trip to Snowdonia. I wasn't on that trip but apparently it derived from a feeling of persecution from the teachers who took umbrage at the fact that our school weren't behaving as well as the kids from another local establishment staying at the same hostel. For whatever reason, the drummer's seat always had my arse on it from the start, which made me feel even more special than I actually was. There was only one minor drawback; we had no equipment; no microphone, no guitars, and most certainly no drum kit.

Although my father was quite keen on me following in his footsteps, he wasn't as enamoured with the musical path that I was heading down, and was never in a million years going to lend me his kit for practising on for the fear of me trashing it playing, in his words, 'a load of bloody noise'. He wasn't mad keen on punk Rock, but wasn't that the idea? He didn't care much for The Beatles either. He thought they were chancers who just got lucky and were in the right place at the right time. True to a point because there is the thinnest of thin lines between triumph and failure, coincidental circumstances that shape our futures, not just in music but in everything we encounter as we go about our daily lives. Meeting the right person, getting the right job, fate has a hand in all this. If Raymond Jones hadn't have walked into NEMS record shop in Liverpool enquiring about a German single that featured an unknown Liverpool group as a backing band, if the prophetic decision of teaming up with George Martin, who was better known for his work with The Goons and classical recordings wasn't made then the path of The Beatles may not have gone the way it did. The flaw in my father's argument is that once you've had that luck it's all about the talent keeping you at the top of your game. And that is something you can't argue with. The Ruin hadn't even got to the heady heights of the bottom rung of the ladder.

We didn't have a name yet and my search for a drum kit went on. But help was at hand when it emerged that my cousin had a set that he no longer wanted. Well that was the story; it was probably more likely that my Auntie wanted the noisy, tuneless instrument out of the house, and this seemed like the perfect opportunity. I didn't give a monkeys because I now had my very own drum kit on which to back up my premature boasts of actually being vaguely competent sat behind it. Tentative rehearsals were arranged to be held at Tim's house in a small hamlet called The Wash, which was about two miles from my house in Chapel, four miles from Whaley Bridge which is where 'Bainy' and Dave lived, and about the same distance from Bugsworth where Jon resided. The house was like nothing I had seen before. It seemed vast, situated halfway up a hill surrounded by trees, the relaxing sound of a slow flowing stream meandering its way through the village like a shining silk thread on a Green velvet blanket. There was never a feeling of jealousy or envy on my behalf, and I'm sure that none of the others felt that way either, and Tim and his parents were never anything other than welcoming and non-judgemental to us, and I really could not understand why he wanted to kill them! It was where we watched John Lydon on Juke Box Jury and listened to our punk records in Tim's bedroom, T.V. Personalities 'Bill Grundy E.P.', and The Notsensibles' 'I'm In Love with Margaret Thatcher' being particular favourites. These two bands especially were not the most competent of musicians and we felt that we were as good as them in theory; it was just translating it into practice. And practise we did. In the garage underneath the house we tentatively embarked on our exciting expedition to rock and roll stardom. Or not as the case may be. Attendance to these rehearsals was optional not mandatory which somewhat impeded our development and perhaps the writing was on the wall already.

Our fledgling efforts of song writing centred on subjects that concerned us, from Geography school trips to the futility of war. Song titles included 'Military Offensive' and 'Political Force'; 'Hell in the Hills'; 'Mummy's Little Pet', which was basically Tim's recurring theme of wanting to kill his parents; 'Nazis Fuck Off' was a crowd pleaser (possibly), and we also did a ramshackle version of 'Religion' off the first P.I.L. album. Our first gig was in New Mills supporting XS Rhythm who were the pioneers of the local punk scene as far as we were concerned, and we held them in very high esteem, almost to the point of fawning adulation. Bill Sykes had asked us if we wanted to support them, so talk about baptism of fire! We'd been together for about 3 weeks so this was a big deal at the time with an audience of around 250-300 in attendance. Not quite Free Trade Hall/Sex Pistols but I swear I was there! We also did a gig in the school gym at lunchtime, of which I still have a photograph of me taken by Mike

Patey-Ford my art teacher. It was a weird feeling playing to an audience that consisted of friends and people our own age, and I felt a mixture of fear and euphoria at the same time.

Playing such a gig also brought out the performer in Jon because normally he would be quiet and reflective, but his persona changed once the first chord was struck. He would start the gig sat on a plastic school chair with his back to the audience reminiscent of Stuart Sutcliffe in The Beatles' Hamburg days. I'm not sure if it was from the pure adrenalin coursing through his veins, but he suddenly stood up, put his foot on to the edge of the chair and booted it into the audience, narrowly missing a 3rd year girl at the front! Thankfully she was fine and we got through our second gig without the need for medical intervention. The gig was well attended, although this was possibly not due to any interest or enjoyment of our music, but more likely the novelty factor that no-one had done anything like this before, or perhaps because it was pissing it down outside. That didn't matter as long as we had someone to play to we were more than happy. We were on the road to a life of sex, drugs and rock and roll, despite the fact that we couldn't play the rock and roll very well; the nearest thing to drugs we had experienced was a 2 litre bottle of Strongbow cider and a fag behind the Art block; and most certainly in my case, my John Thomas was used exclusively for pissing through. Our short history was dogged with a rather laissez- faire attitude to rehearsing, because it was a rare event when all the members of the band were in the same room at the same time. In fact the first rehearsal that we had at Tim's house, I wasn't there although the drum kit did turn up!

One school lunchtime a few weeks later we were hoping to play again in the gym, but were prevented from doing so because there were no teachers available to police the pupils. Undeterred we decided to take matters into our own hands and moved our gear into an empty classroom in the English block. The room was at the end of a corridor so we thought we'd be far enough away so as not to be discovered, and it backed onto the school playing field. This was handy because after we had set up and started our cacophony, the noise was attracting people over to us. By the time we'd finished our repertoire the room was full of muddy booted kids who had turned a clean room of learning into a pig sty. What started out as a rebellious act of commandeering a classroom without permission ended up with us cleaning up the mess before we got rumbled by any of the teachers. As far as I can remember we never got found out, but it was our last attempt at improvisation.

Our best (and final) gig was at Disley Methodist church. By this time our repertoire had expanded to cover versions of Sex Pistols' 'Submission' and 'Warhead' by UK Subs. In the crowd that night were members of XS Rhythm who were looking for a new drummer. I think that I left the band that night due to their interest in me. I'd had enough anyway and joining them would be another step up.

5. THOUGH WE GET BEAT UP WE DON'T CARE

A side-effect of punk was that it politicised me. I was 13 and just starting to try and work out what was happening in the world outside our little enclave in England. One of the first 'movements' that I got into was SKAN, which was the acronym for School Kids Against the Nazis. I was given a badge from one of the teachers at school (this was the late '70's after all) and wore it proudly. Living in the green surroundings of the Peak District, black and Asian people were only encountered in food takeaways and restaurants. I can honestly say that I never encountered racism at home from my parents or indeed any of my brothers or sister. My mother always saw the good in everything and had a very positive attitude which I thankfully inherited. As far as I was concerned, and still am, everybody was an individual who was different from the person next to him. I know that we belonged to one of many youth cults and it could be said that we were followers rather than instigators, but where we lived, out in the sticks, we were very much in the minority and getting beaten up or stopped by the police just for looking like we did made us feel like individuals. As the years progressed some of us branched out into different styles, the each one more extreme than the last.

The ethos of punk for me was that although you were part of a youth movement and it had a particular dress code and a rigid musical template, it was all about being an individual and not conforming to what everybody else was

19

doing. The stereotypical cartoon punk with his Mohican haircut and ubiquitous leather jacket was not my style. That's not a criticism by the way. The idea was to be non -conformist and individualistic, something to which I still try to adhere, without trying to look like a middle aged man trying to hold on to his youth. Nowadays millionaire footballers sport Mohicans as a fashion statement. I tended to wear a lot of homemade stuff, such as pillow cases with arm holes and head holes cut out; dressing gowns; my Uncle's old demob suit and a particular favourite was the tracksuit bottoms worn with '88' pumps. A poor mans' Converse at the time.

Of course another explanation for this was that there were no shops selling 'punk' gear in our area. A few of us used to go to Manchester on the train to buy the records that we couldn't get from Woolworths or Boots. They did the chart stuff but anything that we heard on John Peel that we liked would have to come from the independent stalls and shops in the High Streets of the city. One place that we always used to spend hours in was the underground market which had a selection of superb record shops plus a shop on the top floor selling punk regalia of the Westwood/ McLaren style called 'Roxy'. They had all the styles that we'd seen The Sex Pistols and The Clash wearing; Destroy shirts, bondage trousers and lots of leopard skin print for the discerning lady punks, very expensive and great to look at, but a little bit too elitist for my liking and pocket. Rumour has it that the actress Joanne Whalley and future Smith Johnny Marr once worked in there. Despite my reservations about the overpriced merchandise, there was one item in particular that I really wanted. It was a black bondage shirt with a Union Jack print on the left side, which was the same style as the one worn by Paul Simenon on the front cover of the first Clash album. The only problem was that this item cost about 3 months pocket/paper round money. Eventually after saving up enough hard earned cash I bought one, and it took pride of place in my wardrobe. For some inexplicable reason one of the first things I did was to draw the anarchy sign on the Union Jack. I had saved up and yearned for that shirt and no sooner had I got it home than I was defacing it.

Being one of only a few like-minded people in a small community, hassle was never very far away and it encouraged us to stick together; there was safety in numbers. But you couldn't be together all of the time and one instance that I remember was when I was on my way back into school at dinnertime having just been to the shop spending what should have been my dinner money. Walking towards me was one of the 'Teds' who had a small gang who were a year below us. As I walked towards him he muttered something under his dog breath and just as we passed each other, BANG! I took a right hook square in the mouth. I just carried on walking as if nothing had happened because I didn't agree with violence and sinking to his level. The reality is that violence didn't agree with me because I couldn't fight my way out of a very soggy paper bag. I was built for running away not standing there and getting punched. I was once stopped in the street in Chapel en-le-Frith by a policeman asking me if I knew what anarchy meant and if I realised that if it were to happen then he would be out of a job! We also encountered problems at local discos with the usual gang of Neanderthals waiting outside at the end of the night looking for trouble. I never did manage to work out if they were threatened by our clothes and attitude, or by the fact that we had girlfriends.

MAY 8TH 1979

Famous for 2 reasons; Firstly, the Manchester branch of Woolworths burnt to the ground on that day, and secondly, it was the night of going to see my first gig. The Jam had embarked on the 'Jam 'em In' tour which was a 15 date excursion to various parts of the British Isles. That particular night they were firing their musical incendiary bombs into the crowd at Salford University. I remember the taxi ride from Piccadilly station and driving past the smouldering debris of what was left of 'Woolies' and then heading off into the outskirts of town as if we were on a big adventure. The Records were supporting them and were allowed a grudging respect, if only because they were of a similar style to The Jam. Only they weren't The Jam and when they came on and started with 'The Modern World' it was like being in the middle of a rugby scrum, which was exacerbated by the violence of a football match where sets of rival supporters broke out into a sea of flailing punches and grappled like school boys until eventually they either got bored or forgot why they were fighting and reverted back to pogoing and spitting out the lyrics to the song. Why? Surely we were all on the same side? We were all here for the same thing, with the same tastes as each other, but as I was pondering this utopian thought, the dance floor cleared and once again 2 blokes started a ruck and then curiously, after about 30 seconds, started to turn the wrestling into dancing, and ended up in an embrace and perhaps starting a lifelong friendship which developed out of it.

Although this behaviour was alien to me, a country bumpkin, I was swept along in the euphoria of the loudness and the intense heat generated by the tightly packed bodies, plus seeing my favourite band in the flesh for the first time. I went to see them again later in the year, but by this time they had moved up the venue ladder to playing two dates at the Manchester Apollo. Not only that but the band had been hijacked by the new Mod revival and it was just a green sea of parkas and targets, which was understandable to an extent because of Weller's Mod credentials, but to me they would always be a punk band. I never saw them again.

6. New Sounds New Styles.

The record shops in the underground market in Manchester city centre were like an Aladdin's cave of pure joy. Picture sleeves adorned the walls and it was filled with rows of singles from groups I had never heard of. The best one in my opinion was Discount Records which at the opposite end and downstairs from The Roxy shop. I remember buying Wires' 'Outdoor Miner' on white vinyl from there and the intense anticipation on the train of getting it home to play it on my parents' radiogram/record player. I spent the hour long journey repeatedly taking it out of its picture sleeve just to look at it. In the basement was Collectors Records which dealt in the rarer, limited edition releases. There was another branch of this stall in Blackpool. punk also threw up (no pun intended) new twists on music. I had my own little agenda which wanted to move on and embrace as many different sounds and genres as possible. One of the most forward thinking bands at the time was The Adverts. 'Televisions Over' is still one of the best singles to come out of that time and T.V. Smith was way ahead of his time. Also in that bracket was Poly-Styrene of X Ray Spex who foresaw the advent of mass consumerism through her lyrics and was a massive influence for women who wanted to infiltrate the male dominated music industry, by being articulate and not kow-towing to anyone.

Progression was imperative for me throughout my musical life, the constant need to reinvent and offer different sounds and embrace different cultures. Reggae was a massive influence on me as a drummer and I used to listen to a lot of dub tracks because of the syncopation and how far forward the drums were in the mix. I had also just started to get into the Sugar Hill stuff, such as Grandmaster Flash and the Furious Five's 'Adventures of the Wheels of Steel', closely followed by Funky 4 Plus 1's 'That's The Joint', which I purchased on the newish format of a 12" single, because the songs were coming in at between 7 and 15 minutes long; a far cry from the 2 or 3 minutes of fast loud punk records. These songs told a story of New York (Sugar Hill is one of its districts), which of course had absolutely nothing to do with my life in Derbyshire, but it did strike a chord with me because of the beats, which were provided by real drummers, and the bass lines which, while often pilfered from other songs, drove the tunes along. In the U.K. bands like The Slits and Gang of Four were taking the rhythmic next progressive step, ramshackle dubbed up songs with switchblade sharpness. But before I immersed myself completely in the next exciting musical advancements, I was to have one last throw of the punk dice.

7. Didn't We Have A Nice Time?

THE IRRITATORS. JUNE 1980- AUGUST 1980.

Iris Morris – Vocals,

AstroTurf (Paul Scott) – Guitar,

Starch Irritator (Starch E. Smith) – Bass,

Willie Throwup (Gareth Ashton) – Drums.

The Irritators were the archetypal punk band; short lived and shambolic. They had existed in various guises before I joined, and although there is some conjecture as to the line-up, their first gig in front of an audience was at Nelson and Colne Railway Workers Club supporting Constipated Poodles. The personnel fluctuated as did their respective weapons of choice, with them swapping instruments during gigs using a kind of rota system. The idea to form a group was first instigated at a gig by The Hoax in Southport. Howie Kanes, Bob Booth and a guy called Tony, whose nickname was 'Chinny', used to help the band humping their gear into venues. Howie and Tony were well known on the Greater Manchester area gig circuit. They both lived and breathed the scene and would be out most nights at different venues, because at that time there were so many great bands and places to play that you could have gone out seven days a week and not have to cop for a second rate act. Alas The Irritators weren't even Conference quality but that wasn't the point. Just getting up there and doing it was what it was all about.

They would occasionally borrow a drummer from the Oldham area called Ronnie Wolstenholme. Unfortunately the first gigs ended prematurely (2 songs in seemed to be the norm), but then again playing Anarchy In The U.K to a blues audience at the Band On The Wall was never really going to be received with open ears. A more appreciative audience was to be had on Sunday March 2nd 1980 supporting The NotSensibles along with another band Red Stripe at Cavendish House which was a great venue and part of Manchester Polytechnic. The gig was a Hunt Saboteur benefit gig and such was the chaotic and disorganised state of the band that according to Howie Kanes they had to borrow a drum kit at the last minute from a bloke they knew from another band. It was a Beverly drum kit and its owner was Mike Joyce who was drumming for the aforementioned The Hoax at the time. His act of generosity unfortunately backfired on him when he received it back covered in phlegm and beer.

It was also the same night that the next piece of the jigsaw fell into place. Paul 'Captain' Scott was at the gig and was asked to try to teach the guitarist a 3rd chord, but his lack of success meant that he was asked to do the gig instead because of his superior proficiency. He ended up staying with The Irritators and he was also responsible for designing the posters for The Damned tour. He was tall and thin with gravity defying spiky hair which was held in its' vertiginous position with the staple punk hair product; egg white. I remember Paul being the most musically talented out of the band, which to be honest wasn't difficult. The bassist was referred to as Sid, due to his black spiky hair and leather jacket, you get the picture. He was a quiet guy and easy to get on with, and had been friends of that nucleus of Paul, Bob, Howie and Chinny. The reason for me being involved with the band remains unclear but it began with a telephone call from Nidge Miller the guitarist from Blitz. How it came to pass that he ended up recommending me I will never know but I will always be indebted to him. I hope that I thanked him properly and let him know just how much it meant to me. Nidge sadly died in a road accident in America whilst touring with a new version of Blitz.

The first time I met the band was a week later when they collected me from the front of Stockport's Mersey Way shopping centre. That was where I was instructed to wait. So I waited, nervous, pensive, not really knowing what I was letting myself in for because I didn't know any of the group plus I didn't have any transport for my drum kit. This was a major step up for me and would give me the sniff of the kind of lifestyle about which my schoolmates could only dream.

Looking back now it seems ridiculous that we were trying to get a set together, without direction or even a full complement of instruments, and perform it a few weeks later as support to two of our favourite bands in front of thousands of people a night. I had been notified that we had a gig lined up a fortnight later with the Angelic Upstarts at Sheffield Top Rank. (I still have the giant advertising poster). I also knew about the mini tour with The Damned, but here I was in the middle of a throng of shoppers; 16 years old – no drum kit, no sticks, no idea of who I was playing with and what songs (if any existed) I was expected to play.

It was here when I started to wonder just what Nidge had said to persuade them to choose me. After all they were in the same boat; they had never heard me play, so I was hoping that he hadn't built up my part too much. I'd only been playing in a band for just over a year and performed only a handful of gigs, mostly to school kids filled with a mixture of curiosity, or who basically had nothing better to do. The audience of the odd gigs that people paid to see consisted mainly of schoolmates and the odd punk or two. The seeds of self-doubt that I was sowing in my head were soon scattered across the Stockport skyline as into view came what I can only describe as a scene from the Beverley Hillbillies. A beat up old van driven by an older woman in a fake leopard skin fur jacket with a bird's nest of jet black hair was heading towards me leaving behind a sulphurous cloud of smoke. She had an edgy prettiness, was very thin, and a look that stated that you really didn't want to cross her. This was my first sight of our manager/promoter; Ana Kissed. Ana, whose' real name was Myrna Moore (her husband was called Roger, I kid you not!) had a daughter, Iris, who was about 17 or 18 years old. I was told that Iris was romantically involved with Malcolm Owen of The Ruts, which for some reason quite impressed me!

Unfortunately a week before the tour with The Damned I received a telephone call from Ana who informed me that Malcolm had died that morning in the bath. He had lost his battle with heroin, after weeks of being clean. Ironically it wasn't the drug that had killed him. He had fallen asleep in the bath and drowned. It was a tragic accident and we had lost a great front man from one of my favourite bands as well as one of the best punk groups. It was a very sad end and it gives me no satisfaction in the knowledge that I was one of the first people to hear of Malcolm's sad demise. Iris was devastated by the news. One thing that struck you immediately was that she was a very beautiful girl. She was reminiscent of Annabella Lu Win from Bow Wow Wow with olive skin, a wicked smile and she was very confident. Armed with these qualities it was perhaps no surprise that she ended up becoming a page 3 Girl.

We were to rehearse above a vegan shop in Higher Broughton, Salford, and after being picked up that first day we made our way there. But we never got to rehearse for some reason or other and I remember just being sat in the back of the shop, ingesting the various aromas of whatever Vegan food consisted of, waiting around wondering what the hell I was getting myself involved in. When we did get down to some sort of rehearsing I was still minus a drum kit, so I improvised using upturned white plastic buckets and pieces of doweling or bits of wood fashioned into a stick like shape. We didn't really have 'songs' as such although there was one called 'Anderton', all about the then chief constable of Manchester, James Anderton. It wasn't paying homage to him I know that for a fact! There were two more I remember for totally different reasons but more of that later. For now here I was, getting ready for my biggest gigs yet by whacking the living daylights out of some large round containers with odd shaped bits of timber.

MONDAY 30TH JUNE 1980 – SHEFFIELD TOP RANK

ARTISTS: ANGELIC UPSTARTS, THE HOAX, THE IRRITATORS.

Our first gig; and it proved to be quite a night! The first thing that struck me was the size of the place when we arrived late afternoon. It was dark and the stage seemed to be about 6 feet high. There was a balcony up above the hall floor, and I thought about all the groups that had played there. I thought about all the bands whose first visit to Sheffield would probably have been at the tiny confines of the Limit club, and then after they had got more successful would get to play here. Adam and the Ants, Siouxsie and the Banshees, The Clash and The Jam had all been on that very same stage around about the same period of time. I was now part of that history; only a tiny fragment but one which has been recorded for posterity.

There were two support bands on that night, although I have no recollection of anyone else being on the bill apart from us and the Upstarts. The posters and the tickets only had the Upstarts and our name on them, but the other band were the ubiquitous The Hoax, in what was yet another crossing of paths for the two bands. Also, whereas we were rough and not quite ready, they were far more professional and polished. Even to the extent that the P.A. crew congratulated them on a good set. Ana had experienced previous dealings with Dennis Matthews who was representing The Hoax that night. I don't think that they were greatly smitten with her and found her a little abrasive and lairy. To be honest I never got that close to her because her and Iris didn't really mix much with the bands from what I can remember, they seemed a little mysterious and aloof, but she never gave me any reason to dislike her, after all she was giving me the chance to play out my dream. Tonight was the first one of a series of fantastic experiences in which she was instrumental.

I had my first proper sound check and the kit was miked up. Backstage we had free beer and food laid on for us all. This was another first for me. This was the real deal and I made sure that I got my share of the hospitality. According to Steve Mardy, who was bass player at that time with The Hoax, we went on first just as the place started to fill up with punters. As for the gig, we played well considering that this was the first time I had transferred the songs from random objects to a real drum kit. The reaction from the audience was apathetic apart from a small crowd at the front who were obviously more interested in Iris than the rest of us. This could have been because of her penchant for her minimalist clothing. There were two coach loads of punks that had come from Manchester as well and it would have been quite a partisan crowd. By the time we had finished at about 8.15 the place was packed. This was my first gig with a P.A. system and I remember being quite nervous, but at the same time extremely excited, what with the stage lights and the crowd, who seemed to be enjoying it as our set went on.

The Hoax came on and went down well, offering a far more polished and competently played show. The enjoyment though was not going to last. After The Hoax had come off stage after their set everyone waited for the Upstarts to go on. They didn't. Unbeknown to us as we were waiting for the band to come on there was an almighty row between someone and the group. Apparently the Upstarts were due to be paid in cash only to be told that they would be paid with a cheque, and because of this my abiding memory of the night is watching the Upstarts hastily leave the venue in their white Jaguar with The Hoax closely behind in their blue Ford Escort van, and us locked in the dressing room as all hell let loose in the venue. By this time the stragglers who had come in late just to watch the Upstarts had swollen the crowd to about 2,000. All we could here was a lot of shouting and the roar that you get when there is trouble at a football match or a political march where two opposing sides come together. The night started out living the dream of what a successful band goes through each night, but ended up a being a complete nightmare and a massive anti-climax.

Ana was blamed for the whole sorry scene but I have since contacted the Upstart's lead singer Mensi and he was adamant that he remembers 2 girls being involved (presumably Ana and Iris) but they were not to blame. I managed to liberate a very large advertising poster for the gig which I still have, unlike Tony Beesley and his mates who tried to unpeel one that had been stuck to a wall on 'The Wicker'. I have purchased two of Tony's books, one of which, 'Our Generation' is the first of a trilogy of memories of the local punk scene around Sheffield and South Yorkshire in the late 1970's until the early '80's. This particular gig features in it and has a facsimile of a ticket which I had never seen before. It was a great feeling to see part of your history captured forever in someone else's recollections. But the best was yet to come.

17TH –24TH JULY 1980. THE DAMNED TOUR;

Thursday 17th July; Birmingham Top Rank.

The first day of the tour; Here I was, getting to do what I had always dreamed of doing. Only they weren't just my dreams, they were the dreams of my friends, and arguably the vast majority of the audience who would be there tonight. But it wasn't them, it was me. A jumped up little shit kicker from a rural backwater who'd basically blagged his way into this position. I'd even borrowed the drum kit (thanks Bill Bradshaw) that I was playing as mine had been deemed unsatisfactory. To top it all the band we were supporting for the next week was one of the pioneers of our musical preference, they were there at the start and were credited with the release of the first ever punk rock single 'New Rose'. Although at the time I wasn't as big a fan as most of my friends, it didn't diminish the enormity of the experience I was about to undertake. But as my dreams were just beginning to take shape, someone else was about to get theirs shot down. According to Howie, he was supposed to be coming on the tour with us but was told by Ana at Piccadilly Station that he wasn't needed. I can't remember any of this at all but I have no grounds to disbelieve him. He was an original member and now he was being pushed away. That must have been very hard to take. I remember him being around at rehearsals and the shop and I also remember how menacing he looked, but as I got to talk to him I realised that he was a really genuine kind hearted bloke. But all the same if he said it was Tuesday, it was Tuesday. Even if it was Friday!

The memories of that day are hazy. I wish that I could have drunk in more of the events that were unfolding before me. Now you hear it all the time, whether it's an athlete who's just won a gold medal, or someone who is witnessing an historic moment, they are told to enjoy the moment and remember it for the rest of their lives. In 1980 I couldn't twitter my thoughts or share the unfolding drama on Facebook. But then again if I had have been able to, then I wouldn't be writing it all down now because you would all have known what was happening by the second. It would have probably sounded matter of fact and calculated, even conceited. Instead it was pure, unbridled joy. One of the things that spring to mind was playing on a new Space Invaders game in the hall before sound checking. The backstage area was up a long flight of stairs and our dressing room at the top contained sandwiches and lots of beer, all of which was free and only for us.

As for the gig, I can remember the stage being massive and we must have looked like a Lilliputian version of ourselves, lost in the vast walled city of black booming speakers. My kit, which was more or less in the middle of the stage, was dwarfed by Rat's god knows how many piece Leviathan. We pretended to be cocky though and to not look afraid of the thousands of people in front of us. Attack was the best form of defence in this situation and it was the first time that any of us had been in such a situation. I think we were going down ok but I could never tell if the animosity of a highly charged punk audience was a show of appreciation or if they really didn't like us. One skill that I learned and perfected very quickly that night was managing to move my head out of the way as various missiles were thrown at us, mainly beer. At least I hope it was beer, but I dodged them all anyway, the nearest one came from a plastic glass that hit one of the cymbals and splashed over the kit. One of the good things about being at the back is that there are three people in the firing line when things start getting lively. Anyhow we survived to play another day and the euphoria of playing to that many people was overwhelming, added to the fact that we didn't have to pack our gear down, and we gratefully imbibed ourselves with free food and alcohol afterwards. It was a lot for a sixteen year old kid to take in. Oh, did I mention the fact that we got to watch one of our most inspirational bands play from the side of the stage; for nothing?

According to the White Rabbit website there was another support band, Billy Karloff and the Extremes, although I cannot remember them I'm afraid.

Friday 18th July; Derby Assembly Rooms.

It's Friday so it must be Derby. I was beginning to get into this music biz life. This was a bigger venue and one not really accustomed to putting on punk gigs. The dressing room was huge and it all seemed very upmarket compared to last night's gig, lots of carpet and the acoustics seemed to chop off the end of your sentences because there was no echo or resonance to the place. But this was all academic because we didn't play due to Paul escorting Iris to London for Malcolm Owen's funeral. Allegedly the gig was mentioned on the front page of the *Derby Evening Telegraph* on the following Monday night, and it was nothing to do with the music. The article accused The Damned of vomiting in the dressing room and stealing parts of the p.a. system amongst other articles. There was certainly no stealing going on, and as for the vomiting that just smacks of lazy, headline grabbing, journalistic reporting of the clichéd antics attributed to the menace and scourge to society that were punk rockers. Billy Karloff and the Extremes also left the tour tonight at the behest of their management, apparently after playing their set in clear plastic macs due to their intolerance of the incessant spitting of the audience. I can also vaguely remember talking to a Debbie Harry lookalike after the gig, and she was not just out of my league, but not in the same stratosphere. Needless to say my first experience with a groupie would have to wait a while: A very, very long while.

SATURDAY 19TH JULY; NITE CLUB, EDINBURGH

No recollection of this gig whatsoever. Paul Scott remembers something from the day though. As well as being a very accomplished guitarist he also had a talent for the piano, and one morning in a room in the hotel he could hear someone attempting to play a boogie woogie rhythm. After suffering the noise of the unidentified player's inability to achieve the correct technique, he decided to go and put them out of their misery. He walked in to find Captain Sensible hunched over the piano struggling to perfect the riff, so Paul moved him to one side and proceeded to pound out a perfect rendition. The captain was so impressed with him that he asked for Paul's number and told him that they were looking for a keyboard player to play on the Black Album tour later in the year. So he duly obliged and thought nothing of it until a few weeks later, after we finished our brief escapade, his father answered the telephone while Paul was out. When he returned he informed him that a 'captain' something or other had rung for him and he was to ring him back on the number that he had left him. That resulted in Paul playing on the Black Album tour and subsequent gigs thereafter. It ended when he went back to studying classical music, and that is all he really listens to now apart from the occasional trip back to the punk era.

SUNDAY 20TH JULY; CAIRD HALL, DUNDEE.

Tonight's gig was very special. I was about to be part of musical history. The Damned had telephoned the 3 remaining members of The Ruts to invite them onto the tour and express their sorrow at the death of Malcolm. They advised them that the best thing to do would be to get back to doing what they did best; playing live. According to Segs they didn't need asking twice and hot footed it to Dundee on the train. He remembers; "looking back it was such a caring gesture and is something that could never really happen in the modern day of touring, adding another band at such short notice". Just to confirm what genuine people they were, when I contacted Segs and Dave for their memories of the time, the first thing they were concerned about was that they hoped that they had not knocked us off our support slot! They didn't, and now I was playing on the same stage as two of the most inspirational drummers of the punk era. Dave Ruffy was, and continued to be, a massive influence on me and I followed his career through Ruts DC to Aztec Camera,

World Party and a host of other distinguished artists.

A lengthy comment on the White Rabbit forum captures the shambolic, irreverent nature of the band;

"The Irritators consisted of a pretty teenage girl singer, a male drummer and male guitarist. I can only remember there being three in the band so I am unsure if the guitarist played bass or lead. The girl wore a revealing outfit made from white bin liner material and had an almost skinhead haircut into which a grid pattern had been cut. At the end of their set a female, who claimed to be the singer's mother as well as the band's manager, appeared on stage and berated the audience for shouting obscenities at her daughter. She then proceeded to rip off the young girl's top and stormed off stage shouting "happy now?" at the audience. The girl stood topless for a few minutes then wandered off stage to wild applause. The only words I remember speaking between songs were "Yes! We are irritating bastards aren't we?"

Not to be outdone with Iris's first topless outing the audience enjoyed a peek of Captain Sensibles' penis at the end of their set. They don't make gigs like that anymore! The young man in the audience was Jock Hart and it was surreal to have since been contacted by someone who was in the audience that night over 32 years ago. He was right at the front and his comments were so kind and complimentary, listing it as his favourite gig ever – he even remembered our signature tune, written and sung by Paul. It was a tribute to Elvis Presley which was distastefully called 'Get Me out Of This Fuckin' Coffin'! It was another example of our comedic existence and a tune which always broke the ice. One of Jock's mates, Andy Salvin, was killing time hanging around outside the hall with two other friends when they were offered two backstage passes for £5 each. Andy didn't bother as he was buying a ticket anyway but the other two mates handed over their money. The offer was from 'Ratboy', The Damneds' roadie/dogsbody. He was sick of the abuse he was being subjected to and was trying to get the train fare back home to England. I can't say that I was surprised because he was treated extremely badly and was the butt of all the jokes and pranks, referring to him as bag boy and other less salubrious titles. On one occasion on the way to Edinburgh the band ordered the coach driver to stop, they then proceeded to take the hapless boy over the road towards a small Loch on the premise of having a piss. Which was half true because after relieving themselves, they stripped him naked, then ran off with his clothes back to the bus. It was freezing cold, pissing down with rain whilst blowing a gale. He then had to negotiate a very busy road, stark bollock naked and possibly turning blue. Nowadays it would be tantamount to bullying, but it was a different world back then for better or worse. Anyway he'd finally cracked and the stripping incident was probably the last straw. It turned out that the passes he had sold them were fake ones.

Andy and his mates were approached by 3 blokes who asked them where Caird Hall was. They informed them that they had found it and were stood outside it, and as Andy looked down he noticed the word RUTS stencilled onto a guitar flight case. He couldn't believe his ears as they told him that they were joining the tour after being invited by The Damned. In return for the tourist information the band offered them in to the venue for free and they ended up backstage! This is where they were informed by Ana that the passes weren't valid but she allowed them to stay for the gig but they couldn't stay backstage. There was one guy in the audience who was wearing a chef's jacket and white jeans, and the word HATE written on both items who danced about to all the bands. I vaguely remember a Dutch guy, possibly called Dennis, coming to a lot of the gigs and it could have been him but I'm not sure. When we finished the tour he sent me over some Dutch issue singles by The Flys after I had told him how much I liked them. He was a top man and yet another regretful case of not keeping in touch with people. It took a lot of effort to write letters and keep up with people's lives back then I suppose, especially when you are in a different country. But back to tonight and what was the start of the best time of my life so far.

MONDAY 21ST JULY; TIFFANY'S. GLASGOW.

Big stage; big crowd; great atmosphere, and after our set I sat and watched The Damned from just behind Rat, concentrating intently like a cat watching a mouse; motionless, monitoring every minute detail, marvelling at the speed and ferocity of his playing while still holding everything together like a great drummer should. But even though Rat was a great drummer, Dave Ruffy had everything. He was just as comfortable with Reggae as he was with the faster tunes, especially the syncopation of a song like 'Savage Circle', and it came as no surprise that in later years he played with artists of multifarious styles and genres. To be on the same stage as both these people was daunting but highly exciting at the same time, but not once did they ridicule or pass judgement on my shortcomings. But then again perhaps I was better than

I thought I was? I don't remember making too many mistakes. It was becoming quite normal now to play in front of large crowds and a great buzz for us all, but still I couldn't believe why or how we'd ended up here on the same stages, in the same hotels and on the same tour bus with two heavyweight punk bands.

All that wishful thinking was about to be shattered though. I was woken from my hotel room slumber at 3 o'clock in the morning by the boot of a police officer making hard contact with the legs of the bed. There was much bleary eyed confusion and after hastily grabbing our belongings we all trooped to the hotel lobby to be sardonically informed that we were being ejected from our lodgings with immediate effect due to a violent disagreement between two members of our party. It transpired that Ana was fully exercising her acute lack of tact and diplomacy to a member of The Damned, when he took umbrage and an altercation took place. Who came out on top is anybody's guess, but the upshot was that we were marched onto a cold, damp coach in the middle of the night with the prospect of a long trip southwards to look forward to. This could have made for a very miserable journey, but after imbibing in some medicinal nourishment to stave off the cold, a signature tune, complete with animated actions was enacted several times during the drive. Consequently the '24 Hour Club' was born, and what's more immortalised on record as 'The Crack' on the B-side of the last Ruts single, 'West One (Shine On Me)'. To this day it's still the only exclusive club I have ever been in.

TUESDAY 22ND JULY; UNITY HALL, WAKEFIELD.

Apparently a clipping from the time suggests that this gig took place at Trotters, so it could have been a venue change at the last minute. But it was definitely the Unity Hall because I have a facsimile of a ticket for the gig which was sent to me by Steven Hall who was there that night. Along with the ticket he furnished me with his recollections of the night. Once again he also remembered the 'coffin' song and another one called 'We Are The Irritators'. Iris also made a distinct impression on him as a 16 year old as he found himself right at the front, looking up at a very pretty girl who had forgotten to put on part of her attire. Ana announced to the audience at the start of the night that not only would they get to see The Irritators and The Damned but also what was left of The Ruts, as this was not common knowledge that they had joined the tour. This added to what was another great atmosphere. Steven also listed us as his second favourite ever support band, second only to The Anti- Nowhere League. Legend has it that the venue was the inspiration for the Pretender's song 'Brass In Pocket'. In a bizarre, unexplained incident some trousers had been found and Chrissie Hynde overheard someone ask if there was "any brass in t' pocket". Strange, but true.

WEDNESDAY 23RD JULY; SHEFFIELD TOP RANK.

Twice in a month! I felt like a seasoned professional, playing the Top Rank again. Hopefully the debacle of the Upstarts gig would be put to bed and we could enjoy a trouble free night, plus the audience would get to see who they paid for. In fact, as with the last few dates, they got more than that as the announcement of Ruts D.C. being added to the evening's entertainment bought about a very positive vibe. There was a tinge of apprehension in the air on our part as we were aware that some people would have been at both gigs, and there was a possibility of a grudge against the band through our association with Ana, who had mistakenly been blamed for the chaos that had ensued. A month is a long time in the travelling travails of a rock 'n' roll circus. We needn't have worried. We played our best set yet and the reaction was the most positive we'd had throughout the week. One particular memory of mine, which is as vivid now as it was back then, was the sight of Iris rolling and crawling on all fours around the stage singing our cod Jazz sleaze song 'Stroke My Pussy'. Let's just say that I wasn't near enough to stroke it but I could certainly tell what it had eaten for breakfast. Her knickers for a start, which when you're trying to keep things together, the last thing you need to put you off your stroke is the vision of something that resembled an Alsation dog with its throat cut. I did manage to soldier on though and so relaxed were we that we decided, completely off the cuff, to end our set with our rendition of New Rose.

Everything was going swimmingly until I felt a presence behind me. It was Dave Vanian and the next thing I knew was the sensation of a full tray of sandwiches cascading down over my head and onto the kit. Added to this my drum kit was being systematically dis-assembled piece by piece by Captain Sensible and Rat, starting with the cymbals until I was unceremoniously dragged from my drum stool. Needless to say the set ended in pandemonium and with me covered in egg mayonnaise and cress. That summed up The Damned for me. A lot of other bands would have pulled the plug or got really shitty with us, but they just went down the 'let's completely humiliate them but in a fun kind of way' route instead. I watched The Damned in the audience for the first time that night, on the far right of the stage at the front. Although I already knew it, they were light years ahead in terms of ability and song writing, putting on a professional performance full of energy, mischief but with an underlying element of the macabre. They all had fantastic stage presence and fed off the crowd and vice versa. I was just beginning to feel part of everything when I realised that tomorrow would be the last night of the tour.

I've always had a soft spot for Sheffield. Places like The Limit and The Leadmill became favourite venues to frequent in the following years. The atmosphere was less guarded and friendlier than Manchester, and the people certainly knew their music, which is why there has been so much good stuff to have come out of there. In my quest for information to enable me to tell my story as accurately as possible, I have come across people who attended some of the gigs. The night at Sheffield Top Rank was a case in point when local author Tony Beesley contacted me to give a fan's eye view of that night. Thirty-two years have passed since then, but the passion still burns with the same intensity as it was yesterday. Here are his words;

"It was the last six weeks holiday of my school years, July 1980, and punk had been my calling for almost 3 years. I lived, breathed and dodged school by its rebellious anti-authority code of idealism. I lived in the suburbs, way away from trendy punk clubs and London pioneers - way up north around 12 miles away from the steel city of Sheffield. Me and my small collective of punk brothers were a street gang of teenage rebels embracing the do-it-yourself nature of punk and doing our own thing as we pleased, no matter what the NME, adults and teachers said. It was our time and nothing was gonna stop us! Soon we were all to part our ways and take different paths, but before that time came, there was yet another Damned gig to take in. We had arranged to meet up with local '76 punk lad Bryan Bell, who was a bit of an idol to us post-summer of '77 punk urchins, but he had already buggered off to the gig by the time me and my 2 mates arrived at the local shops where we were supposed to meet. We met Bryan up at the Top Rank and he had already indulged in a few pints of merriment. Diving around to the punk disco before the punk bands set up, we joined Bry to a medley of punk favourites. Following our release of punk energy on the Top Rank dance floor, we wandered around and came across members of The Damned and The Ruts, who had just lost their lead singer Malcolm Owen to a heroin overdose. Rut's bass player Segs was friendly and chatted to us. I got my copy of 'Boobaju' punk fanzine signed by The Damned and Segs and then we wandered around the venue to the sounds of support band, The Irritators. I can vaguely remember seeing them play at another previous Top rank gig. Mates tell me it was a gig of the Angelic Upstarts, but I have no memory of that whatsoever. I can remember little of the band except that they had a girl singer, and if memory serves me right, created a sort of freestyle twenty pence mix up of shambolic punk noise with a hint of the anarcho-styled bands that were to come on the scene. I may be wrong. A lot of time has passed since. I may also be wrong about seeing through a hazy time-hindered vision of the band being heckled and the girl singer turning around and showing her bare backside to the audience".

That certainly sounded like one of our gigs!

THURSDAY 24TH JULY; CUMBERLAND SUITE,
BELLE VUE, MANCHESTER.

This was the one that I was really looking forward to. I had invited some schoolmates and friends to come down to see us, all they had to do was get the train down and they would be on the guest list, have backstage passes, and somewhere to kip for the night. Nobody came. I rang them up to see what time they would be arriving so that I could meet them at the door, but each one in turn gave their reasons for not coming down. The rest of the band had their mates come to see them and this only exacerbated the feeling that I had always been a bit of an outsider in the group. Don't get me wrong, there was never any bitchy stuff going on with the group members but there wasn't the connection that I got in later bands. This was probably due to the fact that we'd been cobbled together for a short lived purpose, a means to an end. That night at Manchester was heaving and one of the aforementioned mates, Howie Kanes came onstage with us to perform his party piece. When he was in the first line up of The Irritators, they used to do a version of My Coo Ca Choo, which was a hit for Alvin Stardust. I'm not sure who instigated it but on he came and it went down a storm, although I don't think that Ana was too pleased, because she had tried to bar him from coming in, but a proper ligger always gets in! The crowd were chanting his and Tony's name, and also in the audience was another original member, Bob Booth. He was there at the front along with his future wife Karen, although they weren't together at the time because she had gone with another local punk, but she came to her senses eventually.

At the end of the tour I came away with some great experiences for a 16 year old country boy and a signed snare skin from all the band members. Dave Ruffy, an inspiration to me, signed it "to the most consistent Irritator!" hopefully because I very rarely fucked up and not because I got on his tits. The end was almost here and as we shuffled off the stage one last time it was beginning to dawn on me that things would never be the same again. I'd had a taste of a life afforded to the lucky few, or the extremely talented and I would spend the next 20 years trying to get that flavour back.

8. Living In The Sticks

I awoke in complete darkness, with nothing to be heard except a deafening silence. It was like a mute button had been switched on inside my head, because there was no outside noise. Slowly thoughts began to fight for space trying to drown out the high pitched tinnitus tone, a result of too much loud music, coupled with not enough sleep. What was I going to do now? I didn't have a job, hadn't even looked for one, and I'm sure my parents will have something to say about that. What time is it? Where is everyone else? The one positive outcome of none of my friends coming to see me was that I got to sleep in a room on my own. Ana had put me up for the night and now the daylight was beginning to creep through the curtains, adding detail to the black silhouettes. I managed to drag myself out of bed and went downstairs to find Ana and Iris in the kitchen making breakfast. I just wanted to get out as quickly as possible, so after making arrangements to pick up my drum kit later in the week, we said our farewells and I left for the train station.

It was a hell of a comedown and the best thing to do after falling off the proverbial bike is to get back on it, so that is just what I did. Before The Irritators took off I had been asked to join XS Rhythm who had quite a decent following locally and it was a step forward for me. They had been around since the middle of 1978 and had originally consisted of Michael Towers, who allegedly played on

The Panik's 1977 single 'Modern Politics' on Rainy City Records, Duncan Mackenzie (not the footballer), and Lloyd Cole. They had formed at New Mills sixth form and according to Lloyd their first gig was at the end of year ball, but it proved short lived for Lloyd as he moved to Lancashire and studied philosophy at Glasgow University and Michael Towers went to the Manchester equivalent. I went to school with Lloyd's brother Adam and they lived at the other end of Chapel en-le-Frith from me. They went on to own the local golf club and later The Devonshire Arms pub in Peak Forest. I wanted to impress a new girlfriend in February 1988, so took her to the pub after telling her all about my, albeit tenuous, link with Lloyd who was still having hits at the time. Luckily Adam was in, and even more fortuitously he remembered me. Unfortunately Lloyd wasn't there but the fact that Adam and myself were reminiscing about past times including our triumph in the inter-school 5-a-side competition, (in which I scored the winning penalty), at least gave credence to my claim to fame. An unlucky twist of fate though was the fact that in the pub the night before there was a darts competition between Lloyd, Morrissey and Johnny Marr!

But enough of those gilded with success. After Lloyd and Mick had gone to their respective universities, the band went through a few changes to get to the line-up that I remember.

A Noise Reduction ▢
EQ ▢ Metal : 70µs

B Noise Reduction ▢
EQ ▢ Metal : 70µs

Bush Tetras — Can't be funky
The Bloods — Button Up
Was not Was — Wheel Me Out
Aztec Camera — We Could
Send Letters
The Cure — Faith
Birthday Party — Release
the bats
The Blue Nile —
Tinseltown in the rain

Defunkt — Illusion
Delta 5 — Anticipation
Echo + the Bunnymen
— My White R.
Gang of Four — 10 Hello Rk.
New Order — Temptation
The Passions — I'm in love
The Style Council — Paris Match
Thomas Leer — All About You
Brian Eno / David Byrne — Jezebel

⊗TDK
MA-R90   1981-84

XS RHYTHM/ RIOT SQUAD/ BLITZ.

CARL FISHER-VOCALS;

BILL SYKES-VOCALS;

NIDGE MILLER- GUITAR;

NEIL MCLENNAN-BASS GUITAR;

GARETH ASHTON-DRUMS.

The material was mostly covers but they were entering into the territory of writing more original stuff. The line-up could have included a young guitarist from the Manchester area after Carl told his Dad that they were looking for a new guitarist to replace Michael Towers, and a few days later he came home to say that there was a bloke who he worked with whose son was looking for a band and was interested in joining them. Regrettably by that time though 'Zip Bastard', as Nidge was then known, had already been recruited. The young guitarist had to wait another couple of years before hooking up with a young man called Stephen Morrissey. I was nearly in a band with Johnny Marr! There goes that fate thing again.

The trouble with living outside of the major cities is that the influential people won't come to you; you have to go to them so this is what we did. We started rehearsing in a rather run-down studio/rehearsal rooms as part of Knott Mill in the centre of Manchester on 35 Little Peter St. and it was owned by Tony J. Davidson who ran the record label TJM, as well as managing Slaughter and The Dogs. We thought that we might as well try to get closer to where someone would notice us or gain contacts for better gigs rather than Church halls and Youth clubs we were plugging away at. The place was certainly in the middle of what was going on in Manchester at that time, The Buzzcocks had rehearsed there and a number of other local luminaries hung out including Salford Jets, Manicured Noise, The Out and V2. But its main claim to fame was that the video for 'Love Will Tear Us Apart' was filmed in one of the rooms. Looking back on that video it strikes me that it was practically palatial compared to what we were using. The room we were in looked like it should have had a chair in the middle of it, a 30 watt bulb hanging above the chair which would be flickering and sparking whilst some poor soul who was tied to the chair was repeatedly asked questions and beaten indiscriminately whilst having various teeth removed with a pair of pliers. It was cold and damp with the brick walls in varying states of disrepair, but it felt like you were a part of the whole scene, however anonymous we were. Amongst the other bands rehearsing there, posters of soul and reggae bands adorned the walls to the entrance and you could hear the faint rumble and thud of a bass and drum above and around us. Bill went for a wander around the place one day and accidentally walked in on a group who were running through a song. The band were all dressed up in their finery as if they were actually performing a gig, and according to Bill the song was 'Sad Sweet Dreamer' by Manchester band Sweet Sensation which had been a number one hit in the U.K. in October 1974. I seem to remember gig information featuring 52nd Street, who recorded for Factory early on in their career, but I haven't found any evidence of them actually using the building.

Despite, or perhaps due to, our unglamorous surroundings, we were quite productive and we quickly built up a number of songs, but as the sessions went on Bill and I began to try to steer the band away from the punk thrash to a more rhythmic, controlled style. This was tolerated for so long, but things came to a head at a band meeting held in Nidge's front room in New Mills. It was there that we agreed to disagree and due to the clichéd 'musical differences' we left the band, on good terms I hasten to add. They went on to be part of the Oi! Movement lauded over by Garry Bushell, who visited New Mills to interview the band, and on the back of that connection other groups from the area, Attack and The Violators (featuring members from Chapel) got signed up. Personally I thought the whole Oi thing was so regressive and even if we'd have stayed in the band that would have been a tipping point. We were looking to move on to a different direction that didn't include Mohican haircuts and tartan kilts. Some of what we had been rehearsing at TJ's went on to be included on the first Blitz album 'Voice Of A Generation', especially the last track on side 2, 'Closedown', where Bill and I were responsible for most of the melody and tempo. Carl gave me a free copy of the album when it came out as a kind of royalty, but there was certainly no ill feeling between us and them. The album went on to be number 1 in the Indie charts and the 'All Out Attack' E.P. did the same in the equivalent singles chart, and they also got on the front cover of Melody Maker. Perhaps a bad career choice in some respect, but

I would have been a fraud to have kept playing the same old stuff just because it was flavour of the month, and even though I was turning away from the music, the punk ethic was, and still is, more important to me; don't follow the herd. There was no master plan in place as to what we were actually going to do next. We wanted to try other stuff, and our influences were getting more and more eclectic. The hardest part would be finding musicians who fitted into our way of thinking with preferably no musical hang ups, or previous experience with other groups. As luck would have it we didn't have to search too far.

9. I'VE CHANGED MY HAIRSTYLE SO MANY TIMES NOW.........

SOLITUDE/ENOUGH OF BECAUSE; 1981-1983

BILL SYKES-VOCALS;

ALAN LONGDEN-GUITAR;

DAVE BARNETT-BASS GUITAR;

GARETH ASHTON-DRUMS;

STEVE JONES-GUITAR;

TIM CLAYTON-GUITAR;

PAUL GOODWIN-BASS GUITAR.

ADDITIONAL MUSICIANS; NEIL PEARSON-SAXOPHONE; SIMON NEWBY-TRUMPET.

Alan Longden was a 14 year old distant friend at the time and had been to most, if not all, of The Ruin gigs including the last one at Disley. A quiet young lad who, looking back, had a similar persona to that of George Harrison, methodically thinking things through and taking in the vibe and feel of a song. At this moment in time as we headed to 1981 he was just beginning to learn his instrument. We would end up being good friends and playing together for a number of years. My last gig in 2003 was with Alan.

Along with Alan we also recruited Dave Barnett on bass guitar and Steve Jones (no not that one) on guitar and we used to rehearse at Steve's parent's house which was on the road from Chapel en-le Frith to Glossop and had fantastic views over the hills and valleys of Derbyshire. Steve was quite new to the area and only came to our school in the last year or so. For some reason he was given the unflattering nickname 'Clot' or sometimes it would get bastardized to 'Clit'. Dave, it would be safe to say, had never really mastered the art of the bass or come to that matter any other musical instrument. He was a trier though and I really wanted him to get competent because he was a good mate (and still is), but when he started to use chewing gum to stick on the guitar as a marker for where his fingers should be, it wasn't a good sign. But I do remember weekends sat behind the kit, which was set up in the window of Steve's bedroom, so you would get the shafts of bright winter sunshine beaming through it. I would put on headphones and play along to records, one of which was the entire 'In The City' album which I would rehearse intensely until I knew it off by heart. It really improved my timing because it was like a loose type of click track. Steve's parents' home was a bit like an open house with people coming and going, and they were pretty cool about it, but we didn't really get a great deal done. Partly through lack of concentration because of everyone popping in and out, and to a certain degree because we weren't really gelling because myself, Bill and Alan wanted something different to the dirge of what we were producing. It was a Joy Division/Cure/P.I.L. combination because we were 'anti' rock music as a backlash to all the preceding years of punk

Rock. At about the same time I regretfully purchased a 'synth drum' which cost about 2 months wages (I was on a youth opportunity scheme on the statutory £28 per week) so you can probably imagine my immense disappointment when the only sounds that were remotely practical were a hissing sound, and the high pitched disco style 'Boo Poo!, Boo Poo!' A total waste of time and money made worse by the fact that I bought it through my mother's Gratton catalogue at about £1 a week over an outrageous period of time, which meant that I was still paying for it whilst it took up residence in the dustbin. I learned a hard lesson never to be duped by technology and flashing lights ever again.

Meanwhile we were outstaying our welcome at Steve's house. We thought that a change of scene would work wonders so we relocated to Whaley Bridge Youth Club which would end up being our home for the next few years. Steve didn't stay long as I don't think he was as committed as we were, and Dave left soon after. He and Bill never really saw eye to eye and it got a little bit vitriolic at times with instruments being vandalised and a gulf opened up on musical differences. The last straw for Dave was when Bill wanted the band to be photographed kicking over a street sign in New Mills. The name of the street was Rock Street.

Not only were my musical interests changing and expanding, so my fashion sense began to transmute from the homemade punk look to the post punk fashion of long overcoats and oversized suits which your Granddad would have worn. On my feet was a pair of cheap boots, partly because I couldn't afford proper Doc Martins on account that most of my income was taken up by my financial obligation to the aforementioned, ill thought out, catalogue purchase. The look would be topped off with a Trilby hat usually worn at the back of the head so that my fringe would stick out and upwards at the front. I also had a brief flirtation with New Romanticism and would be seen around town in 'Tukka' boots with white woolly socks folded over the top of them, and a cavalry style shirt tucked into burgundy faux leather trousers. I thought I was the cat's flaps. My hair changed from a spiky, egg whited mess, to a very short crop to a lopsided fringe style based on Philip Oakey from The Human League but just ended up looking like an effeminate Perry boy. Paul Weller later adopted the same style early in his new career as a soul boy with The Style Council.

One genre I never really got was the Mod revival, mainly due to the fact that it was looking back and not forward and also because to me The Jam (who was the main target of affection) would always be a punk band, because they had taken the influences of the past and brought them right up to date. Not like the copycat bands that were coming onto the scene, who I thought were hanging on to the coat tails of the latest craze. It seemed that half of the western world owned a parka! On the other hand I loved the 2-Tone bands because they were bringing Ska and Reggae to a new audience with a political twist. The Specials spoke about the same things that the original punk bands sang about; youth violence; boredom; the state of Britain with mass unemployment and a government who had left them for dead. The multiracial aspect of the bands mirrored the times of riots throughout the cities of England of disaffected black people and alienated white kids. Although not strictly 2 Tone but with the same ideology, The Beat were a great singles band and had a unique sound, and were not just content to rehash old material.

We on the other hand were stagnating and needed fresh impetus. We were all quite arty farty in one way or another and I used to go to Alan's on Wednesdays because that was my day off, and we used to take photographs of each other in various dramatic poses. I had an old fashioned Zenith camera which was completely manual, and I had a variety of different lens effects. We'd use props such as swords and cloaks, using subdued lighting to give that gothic, dramatic effect. We'd go outside to disused barns and sit in old porcelain baths that were used as water troughs for the cows, reminiscent of a '60's art school film. Once again we used the shadows and the melodramatic sky as a backdrop and we used up film after film, sometimes using black and white or a slower film speed to get the optimum effect. You can imagine the disappointment I felt when they came back from a week at Supa-Snaps to find that they were a right pile of shit.

10. ENOUGH OF BECAUSE

Recruitment for our new musical direction would prove frustrating and time consuming. Potential band members either didn't have the aptitude to play the style of music we were aiming for, or were still stuck in the punk rut. It would be nearly a year before we would start to galvanize our new sound, and it began when Bill introduced me and Alan to two guys from Buxton. Unbeknown to Alan and I, Bill had been trying out some stuff with them, probably because of our persistent inaction and lackadaisical attitude to rehearsing. He had met them during visits to the metropolis that was Buxton, at the Gaslight 'club', which, ladies and gentlemen, was open until two o'clock in the morning from Thursday through to Saturday, unlike the drinking establishments in Whaley and Chapel which closed (officially) at 11.00p.m. They didn't have a punk background but they loved music and were avid readers of NME so were aware of current trends. The guitarist was called Tim Clayton and the bass player was Paul Goodwin. They were older than us and were very proficient musicians, Tim had quite a dominant personality and I remember worrying about Alan and how he would take to a stranger taking over the song writing duties and bringing his ideas with him. I needn't have worried because after a cautious start he grew as a person and as a musician, which perhaps we all did because it was another step up playing with better people. Bill always had quite a turbulent relationship with Tim, but I can honestly say he never gave me cause to dislike him. We started with covers of 'Life During Wartime' and 'Cities' and still to this day every time I listen to them it takes me back to that room at the back of the youth club in late 1981. As well as Talking Heads tunes we also started to write our own funkier songs and delve into the sometimes ill-advised genre of Reggae. I say that because there is nothing I hate (musically) more than cod reggae, normally played by some of the poorer punk bands or older bands/singers trying to be cool. Luckily it was a style which came quite easily to me and listening back I still feel it was played authentically and although I was no Sly Dunbar at least it didn't sound 'cod'.

We booked ourselves into a studio which was advertised in the Manchester magazine City Life. It must have been at the cheaper end of the market, but it was my first time in a studio environment so I felt excited and nervous at the same time. As is the deal with most studios we were paying by the hour so the pressure was on not to fuck up as every mistake was going to cost us money which we didn't have. The engineer/producer was called Adam and the studio was called 'Studio Lustrette' in Hulme. It only had a four track recording facility and we had 3 songs which were well rehearsed; 'This Time'; 'Distaught'; 'Touch It And Feel'. 'This Time' had a very languid opening guitar riff which was a cross between Chic and Haircut 100! The drums and bass grooved along at medium pace, with the lyrics being minimal to say the least. It was mainly the title sang sporadically through the verse and bridge, but the instrumental break half way through the tune was the high point for me. Tim and Paul knew a guy who was a brilliant saxophonist so we got him in to play over the instrumental part, completely unrehearsed, we just let him do his 'thang', and do it he most certainly did! He played an Alto sax and he made it squeal like a stuck pig which gave the song a maniacal quality. A fortnight or so later he was on Top of the Pops miming his way through 'Bad Day', the first hit for Carmel. 'Distaught' was the reggae tune which just plodded along with the occasional burst of a melodeon played by Bill. 'Touch It And Feel' was the high point for me because it had a really funky feel to it with a picked guitar lead on the intro with all the band coming in at the start. This song would stay in the different set lists of all the band's different incarnations throughout the years changing only very slightly, although if anything it got slower and funkier.

We only managed 2 gigs as Enough of Because. The first was at Whaley Bridge Youth Club which could have been arranged as a kind of sweetener for letting us rehearse there. It was Alan's first gig, and my first for 2 years. The second one was more adventurous as it was in the backroom of The Railway pub in Buxton and we employed the services of a trumpet player, Simon Newby. It was quite a decent turnout and the set consisted of a few originals and a version of The Clash's 'The Magnificent 7', its one and only airing to a paying public. Read from that what you will. After that things started to get a little bit fractious between us, so we ended up back where we started with the nucleus of Me, Bill, and Alan still looking for the missing part of our jigsaw.

11. Probably Did, Probably Didn't

MINISTERS OF THE GROOVE. - 1983-1984;

BILL SYKES-VOCALS/PERCUSSION;

ALAN LONGDEN-GUITAR/BACKING VOCALS;

DAVE 'GROOVE THANG' WHEELDON- BASS GUITAR;

GARETH ASHTON- DRUMS/PERCUSSION.

I was still listening to a lot of dub reggae and had also got into a few of the New York bands such as The Bush Tetras and The Bloods, ESG, and the mental sounds of Defunkt and Was Not Was. I remember buying the first Was Not Was album and playing it in the bedroom of my then current girlfriend and as the first track on Side 1, 'Out Come The Freaks' faded out it became 'stuck', repeating the same line over and over again. That's a little bit like the experience of buffering to all the younger people out there. Anyway as I got up to inspect the record, cursing about how it was typical of my luck to buy a scratched version it started to fade out. I was filled with a mixture of relief that the album was okay, but also of embarrassment that a 12" piece of plastic had made a fool of me. Bill was always getting us on to new stuff, plus of course John Peel who had pioneered new artists since the sixties and continued the process until his untimely death. Other influences were Killing Joke, Gang of Four, P.I.L., The Cure, Chic, Sugarhill Records, whilst still following the progressive paths of The Jam and The Clash. It seemed that everyone was adding an element of dance to their sound, with perhaps the biggest exponents being New Order who had gone from the dark, intense sound of Joy Division to a more upbeat drum machine driven direction. The radio was awash with a form of white funk, from the veritable tunes such as 'Precious', 'The Magnificent Seven', 'Chant No. 1.', and although not a hit my particular favourite, Gang Of Fours' 'To Hell With Poverty'. I still remember the quote from John Taylor of Duran Duran who said that they wanted to sound like a cross between the Sex Pistols and Chic! A laudable goal to aim for but I'm not sure that they quite pulled it off.

We had a few rehearsals with a bass player from yet another advert in City Life which came to nothing. Eventually we recruited a guy from Birch Vale called Dave Wheeldon, who looked cool without being fashionable. Most of the time he would just be in t-shirts and jeans but occasionally he'd turn up dressed in a bowler hat, white jeans and Doctor Martens boots like the Clockwork Orange 'droogs'. Dave was a very funny, intelligent guy whose influences were many, but his hero at that time was Mark King from Level 42. Talk about setting your sights high! He used to attempt to play sections of their songs during our rehearsals, and sometimes try to infiltrate them into our own songs, which could get quite annoying. When the tune required a punchy, solid bass line that held a groove together with the bass drum, Dave would try to shoehorn as many different notes as was humanly possible into it so in the end it just sounded like his hands had gone into spasm, so that any trace of danceability was completely lost. At least we had found someone who liked the same sort of music as we did and as we went along we all got tighter and tighter. The songs we wrote were an amalgamation of all our individual influences and stuff we were listening to at that time: Northern Soul drumming, choppy Gang of 4 guitar and slap bass.

Ministers of the Groove, a name Paul Goodwin came up with, was going to be the new name. We did a demo at Out Of The Blue studios in Manchester. We did 5 songs in a couple of days, including another saxophonist called Steve Goodwin (no relation to Paul), and a guy called Peter Lomas on keyboards. Steve's sax sound was the complete opposite of the first demos in Hulme, which was a very high pitched squeal. Steve's was a very smoky jazzy sound which fitted the ballad on the tape, 'Move with Me'. The Other tracks were 'Keep It to Yourself' a kind of Northern Soul vibe to it, 'Go Further', 'Time Warp', and a very quick version of 'This Time'. The recording wasn't the best, partly because we only had a certain amount of cash and time as usual, and I think the lads whose studio it was were just starting out and still learning the ropes themselves. There was a lot of fret rattle from the bass and the hi-hats sounded like they were being sanded down with very coarse emery cloth. Overall quite disappointing really, but it was part of our learning curve as well I suppose. Which makes it all the more unbelievable that out of the few tapes we sent out to record companies, one came back with a handwritten letter, which although it was a knockback, was a constructive critique of our sound.

Paul Weller had sang about 'running to the sound of your strumming' in the last Jam single, 'Beat Surrender'.

He'd put his money where his mouth was and had started a record label, Respond, just as The Jam was nearing its abrupt, untimely end. To be honest I wasn't expecting anything back because it wasn't the best quality recording and the songs weren't anywhere near the standard needed, but perhaps someone would see something in us that they could perhaps nurture. So imagine my surprise as I opened the letter and here was a personally written letter from one of my biggest influences and one third of the reason that I wanted to be in a band in the first place. He started by thanking me for my kind comments before saying how much he *loved* the name of the band. Personally, both I and Bill still believe to this day that the idea for the name The Style Council came from The Ministers of the Groove, but I suppose we'll never know. Anyway he then went on to say that we should consider girl singers and concentrate on the melodies, but the potential was there and that his was only a constructive criticism, and that if we were to do any more tapes to send one to him. I think Bill took the view that Paul suggested getting another singer in as an insult, but we were going to stick together, and anyway none of us were perfect by a long chalk.

Gigs were very few and far between because we were always having trouble with the PA system we used. Bill, for reasons best known to himself, decided to have a bespoke speaker system built from scratch from a hippy in Prestwich. Now I'm certainly no electrician, and it seemed to us at the time this guy wasn't either, so whether it was the recreational cigarettes he was smoking or perhaps a delusional personality on his part, it was more luck than judgment on the few times it actually worked properly. Alarm bells should have been ringing when the date that

courting parents

Reginald Ashton in action

The Ruin 1st gig - Long Lane School Gym
September 1979 with Steve Bainbridge on guits

Sheffield
TOP RANK
SUITE
ARUNDEL GATE

BENEFIT FOR S.A.B.S.

ANGELIC
UPSTARTS

WITH
THE IRRITATORS

ana kissed promotions

doors open 8:00

MON. 30 JUNE

Poster fo
the aborte
Irritator
gig wit
Angeli
Upstarts a
Sheffiel
Top Ran

Poster for the gig at Dundee Caird Hall.
The night that Ruts D.C. joined the tour.

On The Damned Tour,
in Edinburgh with
unknown female

SVENOR CENT

Another one on the same tour drinking brew
for Breakfast.

Town Hall, Wakefi

UNITY HALL WAKEFIELD

UNITY HOUSE opposite WAKEFIELD WESTGATE STATION   phone : 75719

Tuesday 22nd July

THE DAMNED

with guests *Billy Karloff*
AND THE *EXTREM*

and "THE *IRRITATORS*"

My kit at Whaley Bridge Youth Club, 1982
with Bill Sykes.
Note the state of the art Syn Drum!

Me and Ala
Longde
outsid
Whaley Bridg
Youth Clu
1982

Ministers Of The Groove Live at Whaley
Bridge Youth Club 1983. Those speakers!!

Cairo backstage at Buxton Octagon gig
November 1985
L to R: Me, Nick Fogg, Steve Bainbridge,
Alan Longden and John Bradshaw.

Promotional photograph for Chance It!

... and Steve
...inbridge, 1985

Fried
L-R Bill Sykes, Dale Jowett, Steve
Longden,Me, Alan Longden,Mackie.

GARY PERKINS
& the BREEZE

Gary Perkins And The Breeze
L-R: Phill Baker, Me, Gary Perkins,
Steve Morris, Andy Mottram,

Bill was promised that it would be ready for collection kept being postponed and put back. Bill kept going down to see what, if anything, was happening and kept asking for a progress report on his magnificent creation. Bill got the impression that the guy didn't really want him there and was almost always stoned. When it was finally finished we had the 2 speakers and the amp transported to the youth club. None of us are quite sure how we got it there but it must have been a large vehicle, perhaps someone's works van, because the speakers were about 6ft tall and weighed an absolute ton! There were no covers or handles on them and no clue as to why it had taken so long to nail some speakers into the back of a wardrobe sized piece of chipboard. The amp had no tone control to speak of and we seemed to encounter feedback, lack of clarity of sound, low volume, all this bearing in mind that only the vocals were going through it. The D.I.Y. didn't stop there, as Dave has made his own speaker cabinet from chipboard and had inserted 4 x 12" speakers into it for maximum impact. It was more Tracie Island than Trace Elliot. (That's one for the bass players).

Still, we cracked on and we wrote a lot of songs in a short space of time with Dave now firmly ensconced in the band. In between all this activity we went to a 'Battle of the Bands' type of competition somewhere in Manchester, which turned out to be an unrewarding trip but was piss funny as we ambled onto the stage to play our 'punk funk' following the other groups, whose repertoire was mainly cover versions of old songs or ReoSpeedForeingnerToto type MOR bluster. The perplexed look on people's faces told us that the working men's club circuit's loss was our gain.

Bill had purchased a four-track Teac Portastudio so we set about recording what turned out to be three songs on the new space age equipment, experimenting with different sounds and effects for each instrument. The playing was tighter and because we had no financial or time constraints everything was more relaxed, so Sunday afternoons at the youth club were very productive times. The new songs were stronger in structure and also in melody, taking in all the influences we were listening to. The upshot was that we were all pleased with the resulting finished pieces of work and things were looking up. Until bad decision making, mixed with a crass act of disloyalty, ended with abject failure and animosity.

Being in a band is like belonging to a special club, an elite membership which views outsiders with suspicion. Then there's the in jokes, the camaraderie, the intense situations that occur when you spend an inordinate amount of time with the same people. I suppose it's akin to a marriage of sorts, and takes a lot of work to get right, which includes compromising when you really don't feel like it. I regarded Bill, Alan and Dave as brothers, so turning my back on any of them would have been sacrilege. But there was also a sense that time was running out to get some sort of recognition; a record deal or a manager who had total belief in what we were doing and would get us some lucrative gigs and exposure in the places to be seen. The feedback that we were getting from friends and people who had heard our demos was that we needed to be stronger melodically and tighter in our arrangements and general musicianship. To me in my misguided infinite wisdom that meant we should get a new vocalist, who would somehow take us to that next level. I was confident with mine and

Alan's abilities and didn't see us as a weak link in the band, so we would be able to move on without any difficulty. We had a meeting in The Goyt pub in Whaley to sort things out and basically relieve Bill of his vocal duties.

I'm shit at confrontation and I don't think Alan was too enamoured by it either, but it was something we felt needed to be done to move on. Memories of the tone and vibe of the meeting have long since evaporated, so I can only imagine that we mumbled a lot and looked down at the floor quite a bit in a rather sheepish manner. Jesus! This was a mate who we were letting go, someone who over the last few years we had both looked up to and respected. It couldn't have been easy for Bill to be told that he was no longer required by his closest mates, who wouldn't have even managed to get out of the confines of the youth club if it wasn't for his proactive personality. If it taught me one thing it was that you should be careful what you wish for. After Bill had gone we carried on as a 3 piece looking for a new singer, Alan had a dabble on vocals but we couldn't find anyone suitable, again owing to the fact that we were so lazy and had no direction or inclination to make something happen. We recruited a keyboard player called Tim Wells who was a good player, not in the Rick Wakeman mould of a solo wankathon for 10 minutes at a time, he was more Kraftwerk with a hint of Orchestral Manoeuvres in the Dark; minimalist but with good melodies.

Rehearsals had turned into unproductive, wasted Sunday afternoons spent mostly playing on the new table top Space Invader machine that had been installed in the youth club. We'd lost all direction and focus on what we wanted to do, and just to compound matters, Bill kept the

Minister's name and formed a new band featuring the now ex-Blitz bass player Mackie and Stephen Longden, who ironically was Alan's uncle! He recruited a drummer Neil Ward who I knew vaguely and a female keyboard player Joanne Latham, plus Gail, a fine soulful female singer of the kind that Weller was talking about in his letter. Neil Pearson also made a re-appearance on saxophone and they eventually ended up with a brass section, giving their sound a more authentic feel. They went on to be managed for a short time by Roger Eagle, a greatly respected figure in the music world due to his involvement in the contrasting clubs, Twisted Wheel in Manchester, and Eric's in Liverpool. He got them some gigs supporting Simply Red in Manchester, Edinburgh and London, whilst I and Alan were drifting along aimlessly.

They'd got a gig at International 1 on Dickenson Road, in Levenshulme, and Roger had invited Mick Hucknall to come and have a listen to see if they were suitable for some upcoming dates. He must have enjoyed them because even though there were bands willing to pay for the privilege, they got the job. They also opened for Dr. Feelgood and Londonbeat at The International 1 and The Ritz respectively. Bill was now enjoying the same type of buzz as I did with The Irritators, playing venues such as Warrington Parr Hall and the Town and Country Club in that there London. I never played in London; the furthest south we got was Birmingham. Bill also beat me to being committed to vinyl when they had a track featured on a mod compilation album, and to add to that Tony Davidson, whose rehearsal studios we used to use with Blitz, put out an advert in the paper looking for a soul band to record 2 tracks for a single. They learnt the songs but weren't happy with them. The band also won some studio time after winning demo of the week on Terry Christian's show on KFM. They had a horn section and were looking to go places. Losing Bill was not mine or Alan's finest moment but you can't change history and hindsight is a wonderful thing.

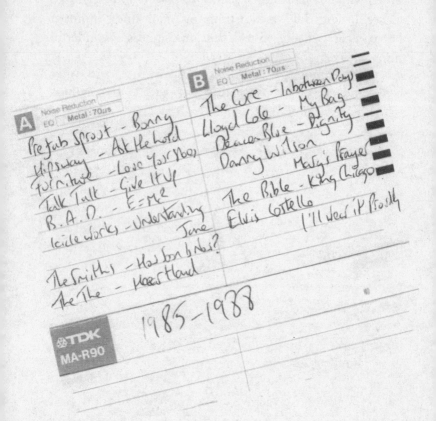

A Noise Reduction
EQ ☐ Metal : 70µs

Prefab Sprout - Bonny
Hipsway - Ask the Lord
Furniture - Love Your Neighbour
Talk Talk - Give It Up
B.A.D. - E=mc²
Icicle Works - Understanding Jane

The Smiths - How Soon Is Now?
The The - Heartland

B Noise Reduction
EQ ☐ Metal : 70µs

The Cure - Inbetween Days
Lloyd Cole - My Bag
Deacon Blue - Dignity
Danny Wilson - Mary's Prayer
The Bible - King Chicago
Elvis Costello - I'll Wear it Proudly

🌀TDK
MA-R90

1985 - 1988

12. This Is Pop. (Yeah, Yeah).

By the beginning of 1984 my musical horizons were broadening again incorporating Jazz and Latin rhythms which were beginning to gain an audience through diverse acts such as Everything But The Girl and Working Week through to Sade. Paul Weller was still influencing me as well and I bought into his mix of Pop, Soul and Jazz references in The Style Council so when the next band came along I brought all those things with me. Also, music was beginning to get more political in response to Mrs Thatcher and her policies. Everyone seemed to have a political agenda which came to a head with the ill-advised, and in hindsight naïve, vehicle for the Labour party that was Red Wedge. I actually went to one of the gigs at Manchester Apollo and came away from it with the impression that I'd just spent two hours of my life being preached to. The aim was for unity in the fight against the Government but it just left me feeling cold and more distant, not only from the Labour Party as a viable alternative, but also from the bands and artists whose hearts may have been in the right place but who didn't have to get up the next morning and work for the minimum wage. The only person who was going to sort that out wasn't Neil Kinnock or Billy Bragg; it was me.

Then there was the Band Aid/Live Aid project which I willingly gave to by buying the single and going to the concert where I bought the t-shirt and purchased a programme. Every year since then we've had Sport Aid,

Comic Relief, and once they thought that we'd got a little bit tetchy about sending aid to other countries, they put more emphasis on the fact that a fair proportion of the donations would be used here in Britain. I have absolutely no problem where the money goes as long as it actually ends up where it should. But that's not up to us surely, it's the governments of all the countries to sort things out, so at least it spares us one night of cringe-worthy 'special comedy sketches' and the ubiquitous sight of a set of newsreaders hilariously attempting an activity which is apparently 'outside of their comfort zone'. Plus if you're lucky you get a knighthood, and you don't turn it down because perhaps you're not as rebellious as you thought you were.

The next musical venture mirrored the socio-political events of the time; management issues, balance sheets, money, agendas, business speak, and nothing to show for it in the end.

THE BIG TALL WISH/CAIRO. 1984-1986

NICK FOGG – VOCALS/KEYBOARDS.

JOHN BRADSHAW – BASS GUITAR.

STEVE BAINBRIDGE –VOCALS/GUITAR/KEYBOARDS.

ALAN LONGDEN – GUITAR/BACKING VOCALS.

GARETH ASHTON – DRUMS.

It had been four years since The Ruin had given up on their attempt at world domination and since that time the other members had gone in varying directions. Tim, the voice of the band, had formed a partnership with his brother Jason shortly after the split which consisted of him on bass and Jason on drums playing a similar style to A Certain Ratio but with only 2 of them, there was only so far that it would develop. They were 30 years ahead of their time though when you think about The White Stripes and The Ting Tings, who took that format to reach global success. I lost touch with Tim and apart from a night out at the newly opened Hacienda and an even briefer encounter on Facebook his whereabouts are currently unknown. Jon never ventured into music even while he was in The Ruin so it was never a realistic career option for him. The other Ruin remnant was Steve Bainbridge. He had ended up, after several differing incarnations, still playing his guitar but now he had added vocals and keyboards to his skill set. Although he was, by his own admission, no Jimi Hendrix or Jean-Michel Jarre, he could certainly hold a tune, and together with Nick Fogg they were very competent at harmonies. I was about to reacquaint myself with him, but this time the music would be very different.

Whilst Alan and I had been ploughing our funky furrow with the Ministers, another band had been steadily gaining a following, playing the same venues as we had done but musically they were poles apart. They had more of a straight pop sound and unlike us had access to a really good P.A system due to their drummer Bill Bradshaw working for a P.A. hire firm PSL. This is the same Bill Bradshaw whose drum kit I had used on The Damned tour. After The Ruin had split up Steve was involved with various bands that were beginning to emerge locally. One of the first groups he was involved in was a band called

Badzillas, which wasn't the most inspirational of names and lasted for about 2 gigs before common sense prevailed. After that Visual FX was his next project who consisted of Simon Boote and Andrew Cooper, who I'd known from school, and also Nick Fogg and John Bradshaw. Eventually after much to-ing and fro-ing they settled down to a fixed line-up called Cairo; Steve on vocals/guitar/keyboards, Nick Fogg on vocals/keyboards, John Bradshaw on bass guitar and Bill Bradshaw (no relation) on drums.

Their style of music wasn't the only difference between them and the Ministers, and for some reason there was some ill feeling being bandied around between us. We would go to their gigs and certain individuals in our crowd would harangue the band and generally be quite derogatory to them. It was very childish and looking back on it now, although Alan and I felt a little uneasy about it, we were compliant by the fact that we wouldn't discourage them. In fact I was secretly impressed by their set up and the songs were quite good as well. I went to see them in Chapel en-le-Frith at the Shoulder of Mutton pub one night and they had access to the camouflage netting that Echo and the Bunnymen had used at the Octagon in Buxton on the film 'Shine So Hard'. It filled the small room that they were playing in, and it looked really impressive combined with their lighting rig. The Bunnymen used to rehearse in Bugsworth Wire Mill along with The Teardrop Explodes who filmed the video to 'Reward' down there, as well as The Frantic Elevators who were fronted by Mick Hucknall at that time. Cairo had also managed to make a 7" single making them, to my knowledge, the first local band to achieve that. It was called 'Seconds and Hours' and was okay but I did feel that I was getting left behind. Alan and I were going nowhere fast so when I was asked to join them, I jumped at the chance. In the back of my mind though it was always my ulterior motive to get Al in the band as well; and that's what happened in the winter of 1984.

We rehearsed at Bill Bradshaw's mother's house in the small village of Whitehough, a 45 minute walk from my house. As soon as we joined, their old style of music changed to a funkier, more dance orientated set, because they knew that was what we were into and it was a brand new start for everyone. We got the melodies that we were after and they had acquired better musicians. Our first recorded output was on a portastudio with a Drumatix drum machine because we didn't have the equipment to record a full live drum kit properly. I managed to programme the drum parts in and we did 5 songs to start with which we recorded at the house.

Although the tunes were better some of the lyrics were woeful with subject matter that included the Foreign Legion, Ladies Underwear, and a eulogy to a barmaid who worked at the Rose and Crown pub where we all used to go to. It was because of this that I started to put my ideas forward and to a certain extent they were accepted without the need for upsetting the apple cart. One subject matter that I was very tempted to write about, but the words wouldn't have got through security, was politics. I was on the left side of the fence, but Nick and John were on the right side. Their fathers both owned their own businesses and they were both following in the family tradition, whereas I was working class and lived in a council house. We used to argue about everything, especially after a few pints and it could get quite personal and nasty, and because it was 2 onto 1 most times I usually ended up losing my rag with them. Alan and Steve were nonplussed about the whole thing and never really got involved. Nick and John always used to say that I was a Tory with a Socialist conscience. I think I know what they meant but it's just seemed a lazy, patronising argument to be honest. Politics aside though, we did have some good times and the gigs were getting more frequent. Also to begin with, the attitude to rehearsals was a lot more serious and we were getting really tight. Over the coming months John and I would forge a formidable rhythm section and we worked on harmonies and melodies quite a lot. Soon we had enough good material to warrant a recording session in a 'proper' studio on 3rd May 1985.

Cavalier Studios in Stockport was owned by Lol Cooper and was a massive step up for me and Alan. This was a 24 track soundproofed bunker which we were to visit sporadically over the next few years. Cairo, in their previous incarnation, had been in Cavalier before and had also recorded at Pink Studios and Abbey Green in Liverpool. For me though it was quite a daunting and nerve wracking situation. We had picked 3 songs and for the first time everything was recorded separately starting with the drums. Although we were well rehearsed I was more than a little apprehensive about being the first in, playing to a guide track and a click track at the same time. I think we ditched the click track soon because I was used to playing with feel and this regimented process was jarring and because time was indeed money (lots of it), we had to move on quickly. What didn't help was that Lol insisted on using an electronic bass drum which was awful, it was like hitting a block of wood and because of my nerves it kept 'double clicking' and we'd have to start again. He also wanted me to use the electronic pads for overdubs and effects which were a little better but if you didn't hit the pads in a certain way you'd get a shock all the way up your arm. Of the 3 songs we recorded, I was only completely happy with one of them, but there were audible mistakes that could have been improved on by spending longer on them but that wasn't possible. Mind you I was a perfectionist so some people couldn't hear what the errors were until I pointed them out later. One by one we all built up the songs and eventually we ended up with a finished product that in the main we were all pretty happy with, even though now it was a little overproduced due to there being too many toys to play with. I still play one of the tracks 'On Parade' because not only is it a good song but the production and playing on it are sparse and tight.

Bill had designated himself as our manager and to be fair he had some of the attributes to do a decent job. He knew a few people through working for Peak Sound and Lighting who provided PA systems and lighting rigs for some well- known bands. Mostly from the Liverpool scene; the Bunnymen, The Teardrop Explodes, China Crisis and also Mari Wilson who was from Neasden in North London. He worked with her on The Tube once and rumour has it that he ended up getting intimate with one of her backing singers who later had a career of her own. He also had the gift of the gab and as previously alleged he was a silver tongued cavalier with the ladies. Or as John used to call him; a big fat beer swilling bullshitting bastard! But he could only take us so far on his own, and the fact that we were broke and recording studios were expensive, a cash injection was needed and it was found with a couple of brothers from Stourbridge in the West

Midlands. On July 15th 1985 we all received a copy of a management contract drawn up by Bill Bradshaw and Dave Griffiths, one of the brothers, accompanied by a letter of intent from our management team; 'The Musical Management Company'.

It arrived through the letterbox on the Monday morning following the weekend that Bainy and I had spent at Live Aid. I opened up my envelope to find an official looking document that was nine pages long and full of technical legal jargon. Now I'm not stupid and I like to think that I have a decent grasp on the English Language, but I was struggling to read my way through it to see if I could decipher the bit that was code for; "your worldly possessions, testicles, and immediate family will be at risk if you are deluded enough to sign this", because they are not designed to be understood by the untrained mortal. They are written in a style that is a cross between Middle English and the monologues of Stanley Unwin. This made us more than suspicious of their intentions and resulted in us not signing it until the following year. We also received letters over indiscriminate periods of time informing us of the progress that the management team were making. Herding cats would have proved more successful.

I have kept all the correspondence between the 2 parties and it makes for interesting reading. The letter of intent basically said, get your shit together because if you don't we can't get you the showcase gigs in London and Birmingham that you need to get a deal. There would be no more money thrown at us for equipment, studio time or promotional work unless we'd sign it, so the carrot that was being dangled was more studio time and access to record companies via them hiking the demo tapes around various

A&R people; which in hindsight was bollocks really. Meanwhile we worked hard at new songs and like good little boys were rewarded with another stint in Cavalier. It was Thatcher's Britain after all and we were seen as the minions who needed the bosses to get what we desired, which was a recording contract. We also had some photos done for a 'fact file' 4 page booklet, which now looks like a primary school project with badly photo copied pictures of us all heavily made up in proper '80's style complete with mullets. Ironically on November 7th 1985 we were to perform the most prestigious gig that we had played so far. It was ironic for the fact that it was nothing to do with our management team.

A friend from school, Val Wood, and former Blitz vocalist Carl Fisher were trying their hand at promoting bands and putting events on. They approached us to offer us the chance to play at the Octagon in Buxton, where The Beatles; The Stones; Small Faces and more recently Echo and the Bunnymen had played. It was a big place to fill but they were confident that they could get us a good turnout. There was going to be a full lighting rig, P.A system, dry ice, the whole works, and it was exciting and daunting at the same time. I was working in a local car accessory shop at the time and the tickets cost £1.75 each and were being sold from the shop, so there would be a steady stream of young people coming in to buy them. I felt a little embarrassed to be taking money off people who were actually paying to see us, and also if they didn't like us they knew where I worked! As the night got nearer we were rehearsing like mad and by the time we took to the stage we were very tight. I'd got the day off work so John and I loaded up the van at his house with the help of 2 of his cousins. We stopped off at the Rose and Crown for a beer and a bite to eat before pulling up outside the venue. We loaded the gear in and the room just swallowed it all up, it looked like the Stonehenge sequence from Spinal Tap, and our instruments and speakers were like furniture out of a dolls house.

We set to work and two of us polished and cleaned the drum kit before setting it up at the back of the stage. I'm embarrassed to say that that was probably the one and only time it received some love and attention. It was all beginning to take shape as we added each instrument and amp and after a while we sound checked to an empty cavernous hall and the sound wasn't great, but we were reliably informed that as people came in it would soak up the echo. How many people were they expecting for God's sake? We had our photo taken before the gig and after wishing each other luck and encouragement we took to the stage. There seemed to be quite a lot of people there which made us feel more confident and we played well and the crowd enjoyed it and danced and cheered. It was a fantastic night and it's only in the last couple of months that I now own a copy of the concert recorded from the mixing desk. Some of the songs I hadn't heard for years and one or two were never played again! Surely now we had a decent local following we would capitalise on it? On the 29th November we played at Newcastle University, and the 14th December saw us at The Jodrell pub in Whaley Bridge which was our last gig of 1985. I felt that we were back at square one again and any momentum we should have got from the Octagon gig wasn't being followed up. Perhaps 1986 was going to be our year?

We started the New Year in debt. £13.04 in debt to

be exact and we couldn't argue with the facts and figures on our 'account sheet'. Technically we didn't owe them anything because we still hadn't signed at that time but hey, why would anyone want to let trivial things like facts get in the way? As for any headway made by the band, quite simply there wasn't any. The odd gig here and there, more rehearsing and we also did some demos up at the rehearsal place in Higher Disley. We were using a barn that was part of a house owned by John's relative. It was ideal because it was secluded and dry and we could keep everything set up which was a real bonus, especially for a drummer! One drawback was that it was very cold in winter and most of the time we all played in gloves and scarves with no heater to give us any kind of comfort.

Winter turned into spring and we were told that we had a gig in Birmingham at a club called the Portland, which was allegedly owned by members of UB40 and that they would probably be there in attendance. Closer to the truth would be that one of the band possibly went there for a drink one Wednesday night two years ago and hadn't been near it since, so that tenuous link was exploited and embellished to make it sound more appealing to us. Never the less at least it was something to look forward to and we were venturing out into the big city. But our affections were now being shared with another group on the MMC roster. Mr. President was a band from the Birmingham area and according to Bill they were shit hot and that we could learn a lot from them. We went to see them upstairs at a pub in Buxton at the behest of Bill, as he wanted to show us the sort of thing that we should be aiming for. They were excellent musicians and had choreographed dance moves and were very energetic, but to me they were soulless and robotic. They had great equipment with sequencers and up to the minute technology, but the songs just didn't cut it for me and it all seemed very twee and contrived. They were very typical of the bands at the time; they had all the gear but no idea. If that was the sort of direction that they wanted us to go in then I was not interested, and thankfully none of the others were either.

I can't remember who the other band was at the Portland gig but I think that they were local so it would have been a hometown gig and they would possibly bring a few people with them to flesh out the audience? Nope! From what I can remember there were probably more band members than audience in the club that night; 13th June 1986, if it wasn't a Friday it should have been! We were in a dressing room at the back of the stage and it was all a bit cramped and you had to negotiate a white curtain which was the backdrop for the stage. It soon became clear to me and Alan that when the light shined on the curtain you would get a silhouette of whatever was in the way of the light. It was meant to create a sort of ghostly effect for the band to enhance their onstage theatrics.

The male singer had a long Midge Ure type of coat that he would swish about dramatically and he kept repeating that he couldn't believe the crowd in here! We all looked at each other quite perplexed because as I have said there was no-one there, if two people had stood next to each other at the bar that would have constituted a crowd. I seem to recall that there were one or maybe two girls in the band. On one song, although my recollections are vague, one or maybe both of the girls were dressed as porn film style secretaries, with the glasses and the prim and proper demeanour, complete with exaggerated pouting, and they were pretending to type, until with a shake of the head, the glasses came off and the hair tumbled down onto the shoulders, and the transformation into sexy vixen mode was complete. But by the time they came on we were pissed and bored, so me and Alan decided to put on a shadow puppet show. Needless to say that it entailed lots of rude signs and not images of rabbits and birds. So as the band was playing you'd get the occasional outline of a person re-enacting the cover of Kes, which caused us uncontrollable mirth, much to the chagrin of our management people. Immature I know but we weren't particularly keen on having our time wasted.

A month later and we were back on home soil in Buxton. Thursday July 17th to be exact and the venue was the Haddon Hall Hotel which had a room in the basement which you access by stairs or lift. It was a decent sized room and cost £75 to hire including bar staff. We're talking big numbers here folks. Once again tickets were sold at £1.75 each from the shop and they sold really well. That might have had something to do with the feature we had done in the local paper The Advertiser, which was read by a few thousand people so it was good exposure for us. We were to have our photos taken to go with the feature so we met up at a pub just round the corner from the Pavilion Gardens where the photo shoot was going to take place. Once again our unprofessional and arbitrary behaviour meant that we were pissed by the time it came to have our picture taken. To be fair to the photographer he managed to capture our insobriety magnificently, judging by the published article. The smirking, lop sided grins and glassy eyed stares that beamed out from the page were only the half of it though. Bill had written a piece to go with the feature and it was the greatest work of fiction since Lewis Carroll. Not only were we "destined to secure a major recording contract soon" but also apparently UB40's record label was one of those interested parties after members of the band had seen us play at their club, the Portland! He'd also managed to get the name of our new recruit wrong as well. He had called him Steve Morrisson, instead of Steve Morris. Welcome to the band Steve.

Steve was brought into the band to give us a designated keyboard player which would free up Bainy and Nick to concentrate on creating a double front man scenario, including rehearsed dance moves. Their one fingered keyboard wizardry had reached its limit and now the sound could be bolstered and made more dynamic with Steve's bank of instruments in the mix. I had arranged to meet him in Buxton one night to give him the lowdown on the band. God knows what he thought when I walked up to him and his girlfriend and shook his hand, because I was wearing a blue jacket covering a purple paisley shirt with a diamanté brooch in at the top in between the collar. We chatted and had a few drinks and I decided he would fit in perfectly. There was a small problem though. Steve was aesthetically challenged and before we let him join permanently he had to perform one small task. Nestling above Steve's top lip was a wispy moustache, an abomination and open to incessant ridicule from the rest of us. What made it worse was that he had shoulder length curly hair. Think seventies footballer or German porn star and you wouldn't be far off the mark. We gave him the half joking ultimatum that if he didn't shave it off, he wouldn't be joining the band, and because he was quiet and mild mannered, coupled with the fact that he really wanted to join the band he acquiesced.

His girlfriend at the time was none too pleased about it to say the least, but it all ended up okay as she is now his wife. As one member joined another was about to leave. Nick had been missing a few rehearsals and it was beginning to piss us off as we were trying hard to write better stuff and get tighter as a unit. It was a mixture of meeting his future wife and getting more involved with his father's business, and he wasn't as committed as we were. We stood this for so long before we had 'the chat' and we all decided that it would be best for all concerned if he left.

CHANCE IT! 1986-1987

VOCALS/GUITAR - STEVE BAINBRIDGE;

GUITAR/VOCALS – ALAN LONGDEN;

BASS GUITAR/VOCALS- JOHN BRADSHAW;

KEYBOARDS – STEVE MORRIS;

DRUMS – GARETH ASHTON

After Nick left it was decreed that we would go into the studio to re-do the vocals wiping all trace of him off them and more radically, we would change the name of the band to give us a clean break and start afresh. After numerous suggestions we, rather reluctantly on my part, decided on Chance It! We were booked in Cavalier studios on Thursday 8th January 1987; A New Year, a new outlook, more professional, and looking forward to pressing ahead. But there were some issues that we weren't happy about. We thought we weren't getting pushed as much as Mr

President and perhaps our behaviour was that of a jealous sibling, but we were rehearsed and tight and just needed to play more gigs. What with being drunk on photos and taking the piss out of our 'stable mates', we sought to make a concerted effort to stop being tiresome and behave ourselves. Unfortunately that plan stalled before it had even got off the starting grid.

Bainy had visited the aforementioned 'Gaslight' club in Buxton one evening with the management team and was slightly worse for wear. Once it was time to go home he was to be chauffeured home in one of the Griffith's brothers' Porsche. Most of us would at some time or other, have dreamt about coming out of a nightclub and being driven home in a sports car, feeling like a rock star. That sort of thing would go to most people's heads if we're being honest. The only thing going to Steve's head at that time was a mixture of dizziness brought on by the excess of lager he'd consumed, and the extreme warmth generated by the car heater, making him feel quite nauseous. As they drove along with Steve gulping for air and trying to focus on something to take the spinning away; the driver looking anxiously to his left to look for the tell-tale signs of an imminent re-emergence of lager and last meal. It was certainly a brave effort by the young guitarist but it was one he was never going to win, and before the car could be pulled over to avert any collateral damage to the leather upholstery and pristine carpets, the gates of Hades opened with a resounding bark, and the beer and bile came frothing out of Steve's mouth. In his vain but valiant attempt to stem the flow with cupped hands, he actually made things worse by increasing the area over which his vomit landed. Apparently some bits of semi digested vegetables had gone into the Bose speaker grilles and had to be removed with the combination of disinfectant and a toothbrush. Respect.

We got more gigs in the first months of 1987 accompanied by our first rejection letter which was from EMI. Throughout February, March and April we gigged regularly but they were all local places and not the trips to London or any other city for that matter that we were promised. Also partly because of the financial aspect and partly because of a spurt of creativity we decided to record some new songs at the rehearsal room (barn) to keep things ticking over and fresh. The gigs we were doing were normally well attended and relatively trouble free. The one exception was a gig in Heanor, Derbyshire that was a benefit for Sport Aid, an offshoot of the famine relief giant that was Band Aid. It ended in a mass brawl and it wasn't very charitable to say the least. One of the quickest pack downs I have ever been involved in!

We had some photographs taken and to be honest they were good quality. The theme of the shots was that we all had individual portraits done, which were printed onto cardboard with a frame which was made to look like a Tarot card. Then all five were put together, fanned out and made to look like a hand of cards. A sinister black glove was positioned holding them, which was probably quite corny looking back but I thought it was quite a different idea. The photos were put into a folder which had the logo on the front and was bright yellow, so it was hard to miss! Alas, for all the work and thought that went into it, they didn't really make an impact on the people they were meant for; the record companies.

On the 10th April we hit what I thought was a new low. We were booked to play at the local roller disco in

Buxton, which was indeed as tragic as it sounds. Here we were trying to come across as serious musicians playing to an audience of overexcited, pre-pubescent kids off their tits on full sugar Tizer. There were a few loyal followers there but we'd told our other halves not to bother coming, because it was bad enough being embarrassed in front of total strangers, never mind people you knew. This was our version of the fun fair scene in Spinal Tap, we just needed the miniature Stonehenge to finish it all off. That week the band had a meeting to discuss what we were going to do to get things moving in a positive direction and various things were discussed. One of the suggestions was to go abroad to play in holiday resorts, possibly Spain, performing cover versions for the holidaymakers. The idea was short lived and never really given any serious thought to be honest, besides that Bainy had just passed his exams to join the Police force, John was going to be taking over his father's business soon, and I was of the opinion that I wasn't ready for cabaret quite yet. One thing we did agree on though was that we changed the name back to Cairo for the next gig. On Thursday July 2nd 1987, Cairo/Chance It! played their last gig at The Chinley Hotel, formally known as the Princes Hotel or 'Prinny'. We used to go there most Friday and Saturday nights after the pubs had shut and it was always busy and as a rule was a good night. I was in there the night that Thatcher was re-elected to power which was the exception to the rule. Tonight was also disappointing and we bowed out with a whimper; dejected and demoralised, we all knew that this was it and it came to pass that we called it a day on Wednesday 22nd July 1987.

In hindsight we could have achieved a lot more if we'd really had the hunger to succeed, but we were caught between the band being a hobby or a seriously ambitious group looking for the same thing. I certainly don't blame the management or anyone else in the band, but we had some good times while it lasted.

S.P.M.C.; 1987–1988.

JOHN BRADSHAW; GUITARS, BASS GUITAR;

STEVE MORRIS; PIANO, KEYBOARDS;

GARETH ASHTON; DRUMS, PERCUSSION.

After the demise of Cairo, my enthusiasm for music was beginning to wane slightly. Events had come full circle in the ten years since seeing The Jam which had made me want to join a band. I had gone through the excitement and freedom of punk with The Ruin, experimented and progressed with the post punk era with Enough of Because and Ministers of the Groove, before embracing the pop/ rock music with Cairo. Now it seemed we were back to square one with the charts being full of soap stars and faceless sing-a-long medleys of songs from the fifties and sixties. There was still quite a lot of good new stuff out there but not in quite the bountiful quantities I was used to. The idea of playing pointless gigs to disinterested people was too awful to contemplate so we had the idea that the three of us would just write songs and record them as we went along with the intention that at the end of it we would have an album's worth of about eleven tunes that we could hawk around record and publishing companies. The problem with recording studios then was that they were very expensive and my disposable income was negligible to say the least, and it took some saving for us to get it started. So we wrote a couple of songs that we rehearsed and rehearsed until we had all the ideas down and booked some studio time back at Cavalier. On the 18th November 1987 we were ready to record. Lol had a singer in mind for us because the one thing we weren't capable of was holding a tune. None of us could carry one in a bucket. We only had the faintest outline of the melody we wanted in the verses and choruses etc. so we would have to try and relate our ideas to them and hopefully their vocal prowess would make sense of it all. We needn't have worried because Lol had brought in a singer who we hit it off with straight away.

Viv was from Fallowfield in Manchester and was bright and bubbly, not a serious, pretentious singer that her talent could so easily had given her the right to be. We put the track down straight away first time which, when every tick of the clock was the sound of a tap dripping coins into a very small sink, was a relief. After some rudimentary instructions Viv got the vocals done and with some fine tuning, we had our first track; 'Release'. Over Christmas and New Year we'd finished another one and went back in the studio on 17th January 1988 to keep the momentum going. The speed in which we were back in, meant that we had to finish the song over two sessions when we had enough money together, and we completed it on 25th February. 'Something Like Precious' proved to be a little more difficult with the phrasing and Viv trying to fit all the words in, and some of the outtakes were hilarious with her frustration manifesting itself in a volley of expletives and screams! So we had two songs done and things were going fine. For the next song we thought we'd re-work a Cairo tune that was the last thing we wrote together as a band, and personally my favourite track. As with all the other songs we were recording 'Cold' used my lyrics and these were some of my best, put down in ten minutes on the way home from another demoralising band/managerial meeting. We had the tune and the melody already, so after another bout of saving up we booked two consecutive days, the 19th and 20th March to record our new version. The finished version was a mixture of great production ideas from Lol and pure vocal class from Viv, and it still stands up today; sparse and powerful it would have been great to have given it the full treatment with strings and allowing more time for honing our performances. Three down and more to come, but it wouldn't be until 23rd November, eight months later, that we started on number four.

I can't remember why we took so long, perhaps it was money because in June of that year Steve got married and with the expense of the wedding and subsequent honeymoon things would have been tight, plus they had just bought their first house together. That wasn't the only change because Viv wouldn't be doing the next track, partly because we wanted to try different vocalists to expand the sound and styles of the music. It was a practice used by some of my favourite songwriters such Bacharach and David and the Motown song writing teams, although we were far from that calibre of talent. Lol had a young girl in mind and so we agreed because we trusted him and he hadn't let us down with Viv. So everything was set up and we carried on with another old Cairo song, 'Stolen Love' which we completely revamped with new lyrics and fresh melody lines. We put the backing track down on the 23rd and Leslie was booked to come in a month later on 21st

December to put down her vocals. For whatever reason, possibly work commitments, I didn't attend the session so Steve and John went to supervise what we required and I trusted them. So I was surprised when Steve reported back to me that perhaps I might not like the finished article due to Leslie's vocals. It transpired that she had a slight speech impediment where she couldn't pronounce her 'r's properly and he thought that I may not have been too enamoured by that. So I listened to it and of course because he had told me it stood out more and now I was listening for it, but it was great. She had a totally different voice from Viv and it suited the song, so much so that we thought we'd give her a go at 'Cold' to see if her interpretation would give us something different. It did but I still prefer Viv's original. That was the last recording we did and we hadn't even got halfway through what we set out to achieve. We talked about not only using different singers but recording in a different studio. The Cottage in Macclesfield had a good reputation and we planned to do the next one there, but alas we never got around to it.

The momentum was gone and the financial restraints were taking their toll, so it was time to get back to being in a band. We all went our separate ways and although S.P.M.C. had only lasted a year at least we had something to be proud of at the end of it. Just in case you're wondering where the name S.P.M.C. came from, the full title is Stair Poultry Motor Car. It was a literal alternative of Stephen Morris given to him in the early days of Cairo by Steve Bainbridge; Step=Stair, hen=Poultry, Morris= Motor Car. Does that make any sense?

Aztec Camera - Good Morning ·   Trash Can Sinatras
Primal Scream   Britain ·   - Best Man's Fall
    - Come Together ·   Lemonheads - It's a shame
Voice of the Beehive - I Walk ·   about Ray
Jellyfish   the Earth ·   The Godfathers - Birth, School
 - The King Is Half Undressed ·   Work, Death
Paul Weller   - Into Tomorrow ·   The Orb - Little Fluffy Clouds
Lilac Time - The Darkness ·   Betty Adamson - Can't Get Loose
House of Love   Of her Eyes · Massive Attack - Safe from Harm
 - Beatles and the Stones ·   Depeche Mode - Enjoy the Silence
                              · Cowboy Junkies - 'Cause Cheap Is
                                          How I feel

⚫TDK

1989 - 1992

SA-X 100

13. Rip It Up And Start Again.

The next 18 months or so were spent trying to get something together as well as attempting to re-ignite my interest in music. The charts were still full of soap stars and rehashed music using sampled riffs of old songs – even The Clash had been a part of the latest marketing ploy of using a classic song to feature as background music that started with someone taking their clothes off in a laundrette. Even the stripper in the advert would eventually get his own record deal. I had teamed up with a young guitarist, Andy Mottram, who was very talented and had been in his own band Pale Vision in and around the Chapel area. He used to come to the Cairo gigs and we inspired him to form a band, and at some point Steve Bainbridge had joined up with him to play a gig in Whaley on the 18th June 1988 with Ministers Of The Groove, which shows how incestuous the whole thing was! We started a band with a girl from Bramhall called Sally and a great keyboard player that Andy worked with called Dave, plus a bass player whose name eludes me. We wrote a couple of songs plus some covers but it never got off the ground and it dissolved slowly away leaving no distinguishing marks.

THE DESIRED EFFECT/HARNESSING PEACOCKS;

1991-1994.

VOCALS; NADINE PLANT.

GUITAR; ANDY MOTTRAM.

BASS; PHILL BAKER.

KEYBOARDS; STEVE MORRIS.

DRUMS; GARETH ASHTON..

Andy went on to join up with my old playing partner Steve Morris in a Buxton based band, Masque. I was aware of them but can't remember seeing them play, and they had quite a heavy Goth type of sound to them, and I knew that bassist Phill was heavily influenced by Killing Joke. The drummer at the time was Greg Boulton and after a while he left and that opened the door for me to go to a rehearsal and see what I thought. To give you a better idea of the clannish nature of the local music environment, Greg now drums with Mackie (Blitz, Ministers, Fried) in Epic Problem, an old school melodic but hard core punk band. So anyway I went up for a rehearsal and joined them soon after. It was the summer of 1991, and some gigs were lined up so I had another set of new tunes to learn very quickly. The first of the gigs was at a venue in Oldham called Club 57 on Thursday 25th July and then on Sunday 28th we played at The Boardwalk in Manchester. They went fine and we got some decent feedback from them which gave us confidence and so we kept writing new material and updating the set and it started to change to a slightly poppy, rhythmic feel. We came back to Buxton and did the local venues, and we started to have a regular Thursday night spot at The Queens Head pub which attracted a good crowd and over a short period of time we started selling T-shirts as a promotional outlet. We went into record some songs at Lea Green, where Alan and I had recorded our ill-fated demos in 1984. This time the results would be more productive and better produced, which wasn't hard really. It also marked my solo vocal debut, when I provided a spoken word backing for one of our songs, 'Common Sense'. We sent out a resumé, setting out our agenda which included some bollocks about rebuking the notion of a visual image being more important than the music. We stated in our manifesto that there would be no photographs of the band to be sent with the tapes! Which was commendable, but looking back it was very naïve and pompous, and as far as I am aware didn't achieve the 'desired effect'. Still we ploughed on and the songs got better and better and we played more gigs out of town, in Chesterfield, Macclesfield and whatever 'field' would take us.

We were playing at one of the gigs in Macclesfield where we caught the eye of Roger Boden who owned The Cottage recording studio in the town. Roger was married to Deborah who was the former wife of Ian Curtis, and he liked the sound. Unfortunately, before I had the chance to record there, I was sacked from the band, because I had been moonlighting with another band, 'Fried'. Anyway they went in to record three songs and because I had been involved in the writing process I was eligible for a percentage of any royalties, so on the 16th June 1993 I was required to sign the publishing deal with Roger and Deborah's company, Amco. My absence from the group meant that I got 7% as opposed to the singer/lyricist Nadine who got a very generous 38%. Also the band had changed their name to 'Harnessing Peacocks' soon after I had been dismissed. So I was free to carry on with Fried as my main focus but approximately eighteen months later I was back behind the kit after their previous drummer had left. There were two drummers after me and because we parted on good terms it felt like I'd not been away. Unfortunately it didn't last much longer and the last gig I can remember was on 8th April 1995 and the atmosphere in the band wasn't great so that's when we called it a day.

FRIED; 1992–1993.

VOCALS; BILL SYKES.

GUITAR; STEVE LONGDEN.

GUITAR; ALAN LONGDEN.

GUITAR/BASS; DALE JOWETT.

BASS; MACKIE,

DRUMS; GARETH ASHTON.

Events had now come full circle; I was back playing with Bill and Alan as we had been ten years earlier, only this time I was joining a band that was playing the style of music that I wanted to play, a mix of Funkadelic; Stooges; and just a loose funky vibe to lock into. The reason for my involvement with the band was that their previous drummer Simon Mason had tragically died and I was asked to fill in at a gig in New Mills at a new wine bar that had opened called Stax. I never really knew Mase as a friend but I had seen him play and he was a very accomplished drummer, plus a really nice guy as well and he knew of my drumming past so there was a lot of musical respect there. Simon had joined Fried along with Dale Jowett and Alan from their band 'Jean Go Solo' who had played the Manchester circuit, and Mackie and Steve had been with Bill in 'Ministers of the Groove'. The mixture of influences and musical diversity was what made the whole unit tick. Dale was into the more melodic side which counteracted the psychedelic sounds of Alan and Steve. Mackie and I held it together whilst Bill would put his vocals through an effects box, giving the all over sound a mix of dub and psychedelia. Bill had sent me tapes to listen to ahead of the gig as there was no time to rehearse so I listened to them intently, making notes and writing out key lyrics and numbers of bars and where the choruses came in etc. By the time the day came I was quietly confident and it turned out to be a great night and it felt like an easy fit for me so I joined on a permanent basis. At the time I was still playing with The Desired Effect so it was a little awkward but I never had any problems learning 25-30 songs at a time.

We rehearsed above the Bees Knees pub in New Mills and it was a productive time with new songs being written and re-working their older tunes, one of which was very familiar. 'Touch It And Feel' was one of the first songs that Bill, Alan and I had recorded back in 1982, and it had survived all these years but had got slower and funkier. The riff was Tim Clayton's and had started as a kind of clean sounding Talking Heads style and had now merged towards a heavier distorted version. I was really enjoying my time with the band and the contrast in styles and ideals between the two made me feel that I was married to The Desired Effect, but Fried was my mistress, a guilty pleasure which felt more exciting and dangerous as opposed to the safe, boring housewife that was so predictable. Unfortunately the wife found out and threw me out after I was summoned to a meeting one night in the Pack Horse pub in Chapel. They weren't happy with my attentions being divided so they thought it best if I left. I know it wasn't an easy thing to do because I had been in the same position with Bill, so there was some karma there, plus we were all still mates so I had no hard feelings, and I ended up playing with them again a year or so later. My first and only sacking

The dates of some of the gigs Fried did have been recorded for posterity on the excellent Manchester District Music Archive website. Friday September 4th 1992 we played at The Ashwood Hotel in Buxton, a place known throughout the years for being a good music venue. It's a Wetherspoons pub now. I seem to remember still having my notes and Bill giving me the odd cue here and there on a couple of songs I'd not really heard. I remember feeling quite nervous and took the unwise decision to imbibe a small amount of speed beforehand, which is not really the drug of choice for a drummer who was there to hold everything together! Anyway the next night we were at Marple Liberal Club and the two gigs on the trot were beginning to make things gel that much better. Wednesday 30th September we managed to bag a support slot at The Boardwalk to The High, who were a Manchester based band at the bottom end of the 'Madchester' scene. Friday 2nd October we played at the 051 Club in Liverpool, a cavernous place which was made to look even more enormous by the paucity of paying punters. We were supporting the Bhundu Boys, a collection of musicians from Zimbabwe who had a support slot to Madonna at Wembley Stadium and four number ones in their native land on their C.V. They arrived at the venue with no instruments whatsoever which created a few excitable moments for the stage crew. I was pissed off because I had left my drum stool in my car and was relying on their drummer to let me borrow his! Another obstacle was that they used keyboards and we didn't, so someone was despatched to find one pretty quickly. Apparently I have since learned that they did have a bit of a reputation for turning up with no gear. Talk about travelling light! We did our set and then listened to theirs which I thought was great – I have since purchased African funk albums, but I can't remember what I used for a stool. Lots of cushions spring to mind and the fact that I was concentrating more on not falling over, than I was on the music.

That was Friday and on the Saturday we travelled to Ashton-Under-Lyne and the Witchwood where we supported George Borowski, who amongst many other things wrote a great pop song 'Who Is Innocent' with The Out which was one of my favourite tunes from the New Wave era of the late '70's. He's also shared stages with artists as diverse as Meatloaf, Teenage Fan Club, Pixies, Radiohead and David Essex. Another claim to fame was that he was 'guitar George' mentioned in the lyrics of the Dire Straits song 'Sultans of Swing' so he'd got a lot of respect in the music world. We went on and opened with our usual warm up 'jam', normally in E apparently. We'd just start a groove off and noodle about with a couple of minutes of funky noise with everyone dropping in and out intermittently, and then it was straight into the conventional set. The last few places we'd played at were at more renowned venues and apart from Liverpool we had been playing to bigger audiences, plus we would get people coming to see us from the Whaley Bridge and New Mills areas so it was a great time. On the 17th October we had a gig at the Swinging Sporran on Sackville Street in Manchester city centre with 2 other bands, Hot Bananas and Loveshake. Hot Bananas I seem to remember were excellent musically and quite mental, and as far as I am aware are still going.

After this flurry of activity the next project on the list was to record some tracks and we ended up putting on a special live show at Studio Café in High Lane, situated on the A6 a few miles south of Stockport. It was a very unassuming place, because it was also a restaurant downstairs but a lot of people did sessions there, normally for the Manchester radio stations: Radiohead, The Cranberries, Ian McNabb, Julian Cope and The Trash Can Sinatras, to name but a few. We booked the room for 24th November and rehearsed new and old stuff in preparation. By now we'd really started to gel together, so we decided to put the whole set down plus a few extra songs, and on the night we had a good crowd in for us to feed off. In the end we picked six tracks to put onto a CD entitled 'Blocked' and had some pressed up for us to sell and send to shops and radio stations. I still listen to it to this day and it stills sounds great. We had a kind of logo which was synonymous with the band, which was a cartoon of one of those toy wooden dogs on wheels that a child would pull along, as the wheels went round the dog's head would nod up and down. This image would be illuminated through a revolving wheel of different coloured light filters, which gave it a '60's psychedelic effect.

The gigs continued and we were back at The Boardwalk supporting Dr. Phibes and the House of the Wax Equations who were a psychedelic rock band from Crewe who were just getting some success and had played Glastonbury in the summer. They were a three piece and they were incredible musicians although I'd not heard any of their material before that night and subsequent listening only validates my opinion that they were better live than on record – the singer was convicted of matricide in 1997. There were a number of places to play in Manchester and a new place had just opened up on Newton Street, just down from Piccadilly Station called The Roadhouse. Since then such diverse luminaries as Razorlight and Scissor Sisters have played there in their early years and members of Elbow used to work behind the bar there. We played there on a week night and the audience was minimal to say the least, it was probably a local band night. I remember the stage was the tiniest one that I had ever played on, and also had a low ceiling so it felt a little claustrophobic, because I was blocked in by the rest of the band and the amps. So all in all not a very productive night, and it was about to get worse.

We came out of The Roadhouse just before midnight to load up Steve's Volvo estate to go home and found that it had been broken into and the radio had been stolen. You'd probably get 99p for it on EBay today but back then radio theft was quite common. The window was smashed and there was glass everywhere inside the car and it put the tin hat on a shit night. Then on the way home we drew the attention of the police because of the smashed window and they had to check that we hadn't nicked it! What made the situation a little trickier was that the car would have smelt of recreational cigarettes, so it was quickly extinguished and the offending article was disposed of through one of the intact windows. The policeman took pity on our misfortune and after Steve had explained what had happened he let us go on our merry, freezing way home. If he had got a whiff of any exotic fragrances emanating from the car he didn't let on.

After the live mini album we went back into record some new stuff in the studio above the room where we had recorded 'Blocked'. Live wise we'd got a gig booked in Whaley Bridge at The Jodrell Arms, a big pub set back from the road adjacent to the railway station. It had been in a steady decline for a while but Roger Eagle, who was now residing in the town, was running it and had introduced live music and D.J's plus good food, and it was picking up. What made it a little more appealing for me was that members of the band who'd sacked me would be in the audience. We'd acquired the services of a mandolin player Vic to play on our version of 'Know You've Got To Run' by Stephen Stills and he'd also played on the studio recording version. Bill must have been going through a phase because we also covered Neil Young's 'Heart Of Gold' on the night as well. The band was playing well and the diversity of our sound was changing all the time as artists should in my opinion, so we finished the recording and I was happy with it, but there were chinks in the armour starting to appear.

Dale was getting a little disinterested and disillusioned with the style of music and was prone, like all of us, to get a bit moody so there was a tension growing there. Also Mackie had got married and Steve and Alan both had children so you can understand their priorities were compromised and in the end, before things got to the stage where bitterness and arguments overwhelmed us, we decided to do one last gig. We rehearsed some covers including 'Song Of A Baker' by the Small Faces and Lovin' Spoonful's 'Summer In The City' and The Door's 'Break On Through'. We ended our days playing a blistering set at the White Horse in Disley and there ended one of my most enjoyable and musically satisfying periods of my life.

American Music Club –
      Johnny Mathis' Feet
Babybird – Bad Old Man
Belly – Feed The Tree
Doves – The Cedar Room
The Charlatans – Can't Get
        Out of My Head
Ian McNabb – You Stole
        My Soul
Manic Street Preachers
      Motorcycle Emptiness

Portishead – Glory Box
Radio 4 – Eyes Wide Shut
Shivaree – Goodnight Moon
Radiohead – High and Dry
Pulp – Babies
The Wonderstuff
      – On the Ropes
Stephen Duffy – Oh Gael
Garbage
      – I'm Only Happy
      When It Rains

⏻TDK

1993 – 2003

█ SA-X100

14. Why I Love Country Music.

I suppose that to most people, the idea of playing country music was the biggest sell out imaginable, and yes they might be correct in that assumption. To be completely honest, I couldn't give a toss. After Fried had split I was back playing with Harnessing Peacocks and we were playing shitholes to disinterested people; that's if anyone apart from WAGS and mates turned up of course. Playing your own stuff was very self-satisfying and noble but there comes a time when the fun ceases to be funny and it turns into one big chore. The songs we were playing were ok but I was just going through the motions and not feeling it, and if you don't have the love for the music how can you expect anyone else to latch onto it?

The British country music scene, when seen as an outsider, is ripe for ridicule and a good old fashioned piss-take. Old people dressed up in cowboy outfits acting like kids who never grew up, carrying toy guns and pretending to be Billy the Kid or Wyatt Earp depending on if you were a goody or a baddy. Promoting a culture that was a million miles away from their daily lives. This was Mexborough not Memphis, Teesside not Tennessee. Perhaps I was one of those people who had those clichés embedded in my head, but that soon changed because these people are some of the most generous, humble, kind human beings I have ever met: a genuine, working class audience which took me back to the times that I would watch my Dad play in the Working Men's Club. But most of all they absolutely loved their music. The scene also provided a backdrop for some of the funniest, most bizarre encounters I have ever had whilst in a band.

DARREN BUSBY (AND THE BREEZE). 1992-1994.

VOCALS/GUITAR; DARREN BUSBY

LEAD GUITAR; ANDY MOTTRAM

KEYBOARDS; STEVE MORRIS

BASS: PHILL BAKER

DRUMS; GARETH ASHTON.

So it came to pass that I, Steve, Andy and Phill accepted an offer from Phill's uncle, Frank Hambleton, to play as a backing band to a singer from Brigg, Lincolnshire called Darren Busby. Darren was quite a popular performer on the U.K. country scene so we reckoned that we would at least have a readymade audience and that people would listen to what we were doing. Fortunately we were proved correct. Darren was the guinea pig for our first foray into the country music scene and I'm not sure how much say he had in accepting us as his backing group. 'Uncle' Frank was the nearest thing to human Marmite that I have ever experienced, and we were to have quite a few run-ins in the future. We had a photo shoot in Buxton Pavilion Gardens amongst the foliage of the botanical conservatory. We couldn't have looked more out of place if we had tried; which we didn't. We got together at our rehearsal place at

Flash and started to knock out some songs, which were pretty rudimentary old fashioned style country music. Darren was a really nice guy but he was quite disorganised and the rehearsals were sporadic to say the least, but that was mainly due to the distance he had to travel so you could understand the reasons for it. The way we learnt the songs usually entailed Darren playing whatever the tune was and we would just follow him until we got it, and soon we'd built up quite a few numbers .One of which was Billy Ray Cyrus's song 'Achy Breaky Heart' which was at the top of the charts in America and would soon be released in the U.K. and get to number 3. Legend has it that we were the first band to play the song live over here and it was so new that I think we learnt it off the back of a fag packet. I used to play it through clenched teeth because I hated it, but we were new to the scene so we just kept our heads down and ploughed our own country styled furrow.

So we started gigging with Darren and we were all a little sheepish of our new musical path. We were still playing our own stuff with The Desired Effect, which we were more comfortable with. One of the main differences for me was trying not to play too loudly! That's quite an unnatural directive for a drummer believe it or not, but one that I quickly got used to. The gigs we were doing were sometimes in areas a long way from home, such as Darlington on a Friday night. We all worked, so we would all try to finish work earlier and get in our clapped out Transit van and get there as soon as we could, which sometimes ended up being quite late and we would turn up, set up, and strike up! No time for sound checks or anything, and then afterwards we had the long journey back in the wee small hours of the morning. Another thing that would begin to rankle with us was that we weren't being paid very much at all, so on longer journeys our thirsty tranny would take what most of what we earned in petrol. It wasn't long before we started to get a little pissed off because we thought that we were being taken for a ride, although I hasten to add that this was nothing to do with Darren, as he was in a similar boat to us.

Ironically after all the travelling around trying to get to places on time the final straw came when a mix up in timings meant that Steve arrived at a gig in Buxton just after we had taken to the stage. It was Frank's gig so when Steve tried to join us he was stopped from coming onto the stage and we had to play without him. Although we used to take the piss out of him omitting the black notes, our sound relied quite a lot on the keyboards, so we must have sounded quite weedy and bare. Naturally we were livid and words were exchanged because Steve hadn't done it on purpose, he'd been told the wrong time. With that bitterness still festering we were told we were playing near Oxford the following Friday, but there was no way Andy could get the time off at such short notice.

I'm not sure what map of England Frank owned but it bore no resemblance to any that I had seen. Perhaps he thought Oxford was just the other side of Derby, I don't know. Anyway it resulted in us getting sacked from playing with Darren and that was the end of our first chapter in our country story. We decided that we wanted to play with Gary Perkins who was looking for a band to give him another outlet in his growing career. But that would have to be put on the back burner for another year because we weren't sure if we really wanted to continue with the country stuff because of the bad experiences we had. Then, eventually it came to pass that after we'd had a year out back playing our own stuff, we got together with Gary.

GARY PERKINS AND THE BREEZE; 1995-2001.

VOCALS/GUITAR; GARY PERKINS

LEAD GUITAR/VOCALS; ANDY MOTTRAM

KEYBOARDS; STEVE MORRIS

BASS – PHILL BAKER

DRUMS/LOVE EGGS; GARETH ASHTON.

Just like Darren, Gary was an easy going friendly guy who had a good name on the country circuit. By the same token we were aware of what had happened before and were keen not to let that happen again. We needn't have worried because straight away we hit it off with Gary and we were now rehearsing in Steve's cellar so it was warm and convenient for me because it was within walking distance from the house I'd just bought with my partner. Gary had recently released an album of songs which were written with his father, Harold called 'Ride The Wind', and we started to learn the tracks off that plus some other regular country tunes.

Gary had turned professional 5 years earlier after his success with his debut album 'Up Country Vol. 1.' Selling 10,000 copies. He was also nominated for the Most Popular British Male Vocalist awards in 1994, so we knew we would have to up our game and take things very seriously; but not too seriously! Gary showed a lot of faith in us and he even had to borrow money off his father for the petrol he used travelling from his home in North Anston near Worksop to get to rehearsals. The money wasn't rolling in from the sales of the album. Eventually we were ready for our first gig.

Sunday May 28th 1995 was the day that we made our live debut with Gary at the Hatfield Arms in Laughton not far from Gary's home. We were all very nervous and I think it showed because the gig was videoed and we all look scared to death, concentrating so hard on what we were doing that none of us smiled or interacted with each other. But we got through it and as the months went by we started to get lots of work including a gig on July 1st at one of Frank's shows in Buxton. Mum and Dad had come to see us and I wanted them to meet Gary and so I proceeded to take them backstage when Frank appeared from nowhere like the shopkeeper out of Mr.Benn, and told them under no circumstances that they shouldn't be in the backstage area and that they would have to get back to their seats. I was speechless and embarrassed for them and so I went back with them, biting my lip so hard it almost drew blood. I never forgave him for that. Luckily this happened after we had played a great set because I was in no mood to concentrate on anything else.

So the gigs were coming in and we were playing most weekends in mostly close to home venues. On the occasion of a trip to Sunderland or Washington in the North East the money would be significantly better to make up for the distance. We had a gig every weekend during October and December, and we finished the year off literally on New Year's Eve at the Pontins holiday centre in Prestatyn. We had invested in stage gear right from the start because we wanted to look like a band, and so we all wore denim collarless shirts with leather trousers, and the obligatory cowboy styled boots, except in my case a pair of Beatles' style Chelsea boots. The trousers were made to measure by a guy in Bollington, and they were so made to measure that it took three goes to get Gary's to fit! We certainly got some mileage out of them that's for sure. So we looked the part and to keep the professionalism aspect going we had a policy that we would take it in turns to drive and that the three who were drinking didn't touch a drop until the beginning of the last set. This lasted for a while and then we decided that perhaps after the first set would be okay to start as long as it was only one. Then it went to two, three might be alright but four was pushing it and five was suicidal! Luckily it never got that far. The poor person who was driving would invariably end up having to stop the van for pee breaks on the way home, as well as having to endure the drunken, nonsensical behaviour completely tee total because we had a serious pact that whoever drove didn't even have a sip of alcohol, and we stuck to that mantra all throughout the life of the band.

By the start of 1996 we had 54 gigs booked already for that year so we were travelling and playing nearly every weekend. I'd just moved to Buxton and my partner was a gig widow to such an extent that one of a new circle of friends we had started to go out with never realised she had a partner for the first six months of them knowing her! The workload was beginning to spell trouble for our poor old Transit van and after a couple of months the old girl decided that enough was enough and on March 16th we left a gig at a small village called Sutton St. Edmunds near Spalding in Lincolnshire, and just as we had begun climbing a steep hill the clutch went bang. Luckily we were in the AA so after an hour or two we thought that a car transporter would come and take us home, but what turned up was just a normal van which was of no use whatsoever. Eventually after another couple of hours we were loaded onto the back of the lorry and we all went into the cab thoroughly pissed off. What compounded our misery was the fact that Phill had booked the Bruno/ Tyson fight on box office and we were going to miss it live, but he'd had the foresight to set it up so it was being recorded as a back up. There was beer and food sorted and we were really looking forward to cheering Frank on to victory. So in true The Likely Lads style the journey back was spent telling the driver not to put the radio on or tell us what the result was, because we would be watching it when we got back. We arrived back at Phill's just before 8 am and after we'd made sure that the fight had recorded properly, we switched the telly on just in time to see the 8 o'clock news footage of Bruno hitting the deck! The beer remained undrunk and I had just lost my appetite. So Steve and I trudged off home thoroughly dejected. I suppose sometimes you just have to accept that it's just not your day.

To try and describe the sounds and smells of a Transit van containing four blokes, sometimes travelling for 3-4 hours is not easy unless you have lived through it yourself. We used a rota system for the designated driver duties which meant we'd all be able to have a beer 3 times in every 4 gigs. Andy normally drove the van to the venue mainly because it was parked at his Mum and Dad's house. Picking up the rest of us on the way we would make the obligatory stop off at the off licence for the night's alcohol prescription. When possible we'd use a shop in Buxton which usually sold off slightly out of date cans at a very cheap rate. We are all still here to tell the tale so the long term effects didn't manifest themselves into anything serious, but the short term effects proved to be an altogether different kettle of fish. A short time into the journey and after the usual inane conversation and piss taking banter, predominantly at Andy's expense, the farting would start. Whoever it was who started the gaseous proceedings wasn't important because then it would become a fiercely competitive competition to see who could create the most odious and vile stench. There were different categories such as the violent silent ones which without an aural warning, the odour would wrap around your throat and seep into your nostrils before you had time to reach for the window handle or bury your face into your sleeve. This method was my particular weapon of choice because it was the element of surprise which resulted in the other's contorted faces, and the fact that there was no time to nullify the attack. Marks were given on presentation, content, and sound, which meant that in the quest for the perfect ten, risks of a literal backfire were greatly enhanced. The person who endured most of the nasal torture was the driver because he had to keep at least one hand on the wheel. The only other real partial escape or temporary respite came from hanging their head out of the window. At that particular moment in time breathing in Carbon Monoxide outside, was infinitely preferable to ingesting the methane cloud inside. The triumphant winner could feel smug with self-satisfaction at putting his fellow band members into a state of mind altering biliousness. That winner more often than not was Steve. The question we would ask him when he got into the back of the van was what he'd had to eat, or what he'd brought with him to eat. Eggs, baked beans, and an array of vegetables was the usual response which, if we were travelling to Norfolk meant that by the time we'd reached the A47 the childish mirth of toilet humour, and even the begrudging respect, had turned into an overwhelming appetite for murder as wave after wave of noxious emissions emanated from his overactive bowels. We were trapped in a white van hell and it felt like we were bleeding hydrochloric acid from every orifice, and a slither of barbed wire was lodged stuck in our throats. He was one of the few people that I have met who could make a fly sick.

Sometimes though, the last thing I wanted to do was to get in a van and travel miles to entertain people. The worst times were if you'd had a crap day at work and you just wanted to get home, put the telly on and crack open a beer. If it was a weekend and the sun was shining or I wanted to go to watch Derby play it was a chore and would result in a shitty mood. However after about 10 minutes in the van the mickey taking would start, there would be a tape of tunes on the cassette player and the mood would lift. We all had a good sense of humour and didn't take ourselves too seriously. One day we were on our travels and had stopped at some traffic lights. As we sat there waiting for them to change we noticed the muffled thud of a repetitive bass drum. Pulled up alongside us were a couple of lads in their pride and joy; Corsa/Fiesta/Saxo, delete as applicable. We wound down the window to be confronted with a 'tune' that was blaring out from their tin can. After exchanged grudging looks with them Phill reached over to the radio and proceeded to turn it up to its' full ear splitting, speaker distorting volume, drowning out their drum 'n' bass in favour of Ronan Keating's 'Life Is A Rollercoaster'. We pulled away from the lights pissing ourselves laughing as they stalled the car and were left behind, perplexed and embarrassed.

Because of the amount of gigs we were doing there were occasions where we would have a mini tour incorporating Friday, Saturday, and Sunday. If we were playing at a Pontins or Haven camp then we'd have chalet in which we all slept in, but sometimes it was a case of anywhere you can lay your head. One night we were stopping over at 'Maureen's Place' near to Cheltenham and because we had another gig on the Saturday it made sense to stop there. So Gary slept in the van with Andy and Heidi, his wife to be. Phill slept in Gary's car for reasons that will be explained shortly, so that left me and Steve with nowhere to sleep. We used our initiative and took the cardboard P.A. speaker covers off and crawled inside them. They were nearly six feet high and were quite robust and they had square holes cut out in them so you could access the carrying handles. So there we were lying side by side and grinning like stupid schoolboys at each other through the holes, and it was a warm night so everything seemed fine. We woke up the next morning covered in earwigs as well as other insects, absolutely freezing cold with a banging hangover to match.

We all slept with one another at some time during our existence except for Phill, because he didn't just snore, he rattled the windows out and you could hear him even if you were two doors down. For whatever reason, one night I ended up in a room with him at a Formule One hotel near Doncaster. I lasted about 10 minutes and it was either smother him with a pillow or find somewhere else to sleep. Believe me he'd take some smothering, so alternative arrangements had to be made. These 'hotels' originated in France and they were cheap and very clean but quite basic. All the other rooms were taken so I ended up trying to sleep in the communal shower room, hoping that no-one needed to use it during the night. I was in the foetal position crammed into the driest of the shower cubicles that I could find, down the corridor from my comfortable bed but I could still hear him snorting and rattling the place to bits! I think I managed a couple of hours and spent the next day very tired and extremely grumpy.

One trip that was enjoyable was our weekend away on Shetland and the surrounding islands. We were invited up by Shona and her husband who ran the music club there and we would be staying at their house. We flew from Manchester to Aberdeen on Friday 17th May, and then from Aberdeen we made it to Lerwick on what seemed like a First World War bi-plane. The video footage that was taken by Gary as we walked to the terminus shows the relief in our faces as we waved to an imaginary crowd in pure Beatles/JFK style. For some reason I was carrying my bass drum pedal in my hand which sort of spoilt the illusion somewhat. I don't remember seeing any footage of Ringo carrying a piece of hardware from his kit. Once we were settled in we were to play three gigs; two at the Country Music Club on Friday and Sunday night, and sandwiched in between these was a curious night on the island of Whalsay to the North East of Lerwick. It was about an hour long choppy ferry ride away from the mainland and is still one of the most barren places that I have visited. On the way over we took our minds off our lack of sea legs by the usual sport of taking the piss out of Andy. He'd recently got divorced and was now single and free to mingle, so we decided to tell everyone we came across that he was gay. Very childish and not politically correct, but very funny, and one of those we told was the captain of our ferry. He either didn't fancy him or couldn't tell a blind word we were saying because he just looked at us as if we were mentally unstable. The gig was a tense affair with no atmosphere and we didn't really enjoy it, so the only thing to do was to drink ourselves into oblivion. The one constant theme we experienced was that the Shetlanders like to party and sleep was optional, if not frowned upon, so when in Rome....!

Something else that became apparent to us was that it never really got dark. I've got video footage of me and Andy stood outside in Shona's garden at about 4 o'clock in the morning looking out to sea and you could see for miles. To add to the time related confusion you can hear me on the tape exclaiming that people were still turning up at the house! One night we all went back to someone's flat for more talking and drinking, but nobody really knew where it was because we'd gone straight there from the gig. Eventually I crashed on the floor and Phill decided he wanted a comfortable bed so decided to go back to Shona's house. He'd managed to find a taxi and proceeded to drunkenly instruct the driver to take him to Shona's.

Now I know that they are a close knit community but thinking that the taxi driver will; a) know everyone by name, and b) also know where that particular individual lived, was stretching it a bit. After driving around for about 15 minutes whilst pacifying the driver by explaining that he would recognise the house when he saw it, he got out after recognising a land mark which was near where he wanted to be. It was about 500 yards from where he'd got into it! And so £20 and one bemused taxi driver later he did eventually get back to Shona's.

On the Monday morning we headed back to the airport to begin our trip back home. We were a little pensive at having to endure another buttock clenching ride in a Gypsy Moth, but something happened on the way back which took our minds off it. The guy driving us back was a very serious and surly guy from what I remember and Phill was doing his usual trick of making conversation but was getting nowhere, much to our amusement. So after a prolonged silence this guy made a very strange noise that was a cross between a stifled cough and a grunt. That was all we needed to start echoing our own sounds one by one, and after about two minutes of this I was crying uncontrollably with my head pressed against the front side window, facing away from the driver, shaking like a shitting dog. Whether or not he had cottoned onto to our piss taking I don't know but I apologise unreservedly now for our infantile behaviour. Our laughter soon turned to dread as we boarded the plane to Aberdeen and then from Aberdeen to Manchester. We numbed our fear by drinking the plane dry of Smirnoff Blue Vodka miniatures and made an impression on one of the hostesses who ended up coming to see us at one of our gigs a few weeks later.

15. THERE IS A LIGHT THAT NEVER GOES OUT.

On 31st October 1996 my father passed away. He had been fighting cancer for several years and in that time he had unwillingly donated one of his testicles and his left eye to the disease. But cancer has a voracious appetite and it continued to spread its poisonous tentacles until it found his liver. Its work was done now and there was nothing anyone could do. I received a telephone call at work and it was Mum and she handed the telephone to my Dad once she knew it was me she was talking to. "I've got something to tell you but don't be worried" he said. Before I could start processing my thoughts as to the reason for the call he explained very calmly. "I've just come back from the Hospital and it's in my Liver". I knew what 'It' meant and again before I could reply he repeated his instruction for me not to worry and that he'd see me when I got home from work. I didn't cry; I didn't do anything; it was as if his calmness and matter of fact explanation had transmitted itself through to me. I just put the phone down and carried on with my work.

A couple of weeks later and I still hadn't told my partner Ann about my Dad's condition. One night while I was upstairs getting changed to go out he must have told her because on the way down to the pub she broke down. She couldn't understand how I could be so calm about it all, but within seconds I was sobbing until I couldn't breathe properly. God knows what people would have thought when they saw us both in floods of tears outside the pub. As the weeks passed you could see him getting older and more drawn. We'd just bought a house in September and that took my mind off things for short periods, but the days that passed without seeing him only exacerbated the speed in which he was slipping away. He never got to visit the house. Mum didn't want him to go into a hospice and cared for him at home with the help of her sisters and the Macmillan nurses who would make things as normal and comfortable as possible. She'd set a bed up in the front room and that was where he would lie, still and occasionally crying with pain as the effects of the drugs wore off and he could feel his bones burning and aching. This avaricious plague that deems it insufficient to just turn your physical being into a hollow shell, also contaminates every ounce of dignity there is left, and for those it doesn't (yet) infect it manifests itself as bitterness. This bastard disease. Why don't people who murder children or torture animals get it? Why do all the good people get it? Where is the justice in its selection process? How can someone justify a footballer being paid hundreds of thousands of pounds a week when these wonderful nurses get paid a relative pittance? I hope that nobody has to go through the task of lifting a parent from their bed, trying desperately not to hold on too tight because their bones feel like brittle paper that would crush into dust, lifting them onto a commode where they face the ignominy of being treated like baby, watching them dissolve over time like sand in an hourglass – it is a painful process. But resentment and rancour will only eat away at you if you let it, so it's best not to dwell on it.

When he was finally relieved of all of his suffering there was a sense of comfort that he wasn't hurting anymore and he'd succumbed to the sleep of the just. It's only later, sometimes years later, that you fully appreciate the magnitude of the death of a parent. I'd inherited so much from him, my sense of humour, an outlook on taking one day at a time and living it like it was your last. Even now my biggest bug bear is with people who waste time. You have to use every second to do and see as much as you can. The best thing he gave me was the gift of music. That's one of the best gifts you can give anyone.

16. Television's Over.

At the end of 1996 we were nominated for the best British band in the U.K country music awards. We didn't win but it was a great reward for all our hard work during the rest of the year. 1997 was looking just as busy and we also decided that we would record an album on the back of our growing reputation. In May we released 'Free To Love' which included some covers, some of Gary's songs reworked and the title track written by Andy with lyrics by Gary. It was recorded in Chesterfield in a studio situated in a courtyard at the back of the Winding Wheel music venue. One day we'd come outside for some fresh air and Elkie Brooks, who was playing at The Wheel that night, was outside the backstage area smoking a cigarette. We exchanged a nodding of heads and went back inside. We also embarked on a video of one of the songs off it called 'Five String Guitar', which started off okay but degenerated into drunken chaos. The story line followed the lyrics of the song that told the tale of when Gary was in Greece and he'd got up to play some tunes, in return for free beer on an old guitar that, you guessed it, only had five strings. So our visual interpretation consisted of me and Steve buying a beer off Phill who played the barman. So crap were our acting skills that we needed about 6 takes to get it right and in sync with the backing track. So instead of using the same bottle each time, or God forbid 'pretending' to drink something, we cracked a new bottle open for each take!

To make matters slightly worse the alcohol was out of date stuff that we'd got from our cheap dealer. We were quite merry by the time we'd got the 'wrap', to the extent that I ended up falling off a toy bike and getting severe gravel rash of the knee whilst we murdered another 'hilarious' scene. I've never seen the full edited version and that's probably a good thing.

The album did really well and we signed to a label in America called Comstock Records from Arizona and they put a track off the album, 'Thunderhead' on their sampler compact disc that got air play all over Europe in Sweden, Spain, Holland, Belgium and France. We also went back to the Shetlands in January '97 but the people seemed more subdued than before because things were getting tough financially there as they were in the rest of the U.K. But to make it better we were voted the best band to have played there last year and we all received silver lapel pins of a cowboy hat which I still have in its box and very proud of it I am too. We won more awards that year and Gary was successful with his solo stuff as well. One thing that was helping to fill the clubs at first was the latest craze of Line Dancing. Some traditionalists hated it and thought that it spelt the death of live music, because why pay a full band when you only needed to get yourself a D.J.? We ended up embracing it and sometimes we would get a little pissed off because the audience wouldn't know our own written material and so couldn't dance to it, and other times we'd be seen as a minor irritant in between the D.J. spots. But in the end we had people writing dances for our songs and for a while we rode with it. In fact it was partly through popularity in the media of the dance craze that we were invited to appear on a live broadcast on television in the summer.

This was my second experience with the magical world of television and was completely different and a lot more nerve wracking. On August 8th 1997 we had managed to get a slot on the early evening local news and events programme Calendar which catered primarily to the Yorkshire area. According to people in the know the show's viewing figures were on average over a million and this particular edition of the programme was a summer special outside broadcast from the Doncaster Dome as part of their county wide road show, taking in different parts of the region every week. Our reason for being there was that the programme had a feature on a new Country music only radio station in the area. Gary had done gigs for them in the past and they liked the band, so here we were.

We arrived early morning as instructed. The show started at 6.00pm and we needed to set up, sound check and get the camera positions and sequences practised. It was a beautiful day thankfully because we were open to the elements, and rain was not an option. On top of the luck with the good weather we were also given free reign at the Dome, which meant swimming, and food and drinks all free of charge. Success certainly gets you places! The sound check went well and after numerous run throughs, the production team got all its' angles and shots finalised; everything was all going to plan. Except for one thing; Gary was not well. He'd been suffering from Campylobacter, an intestinal disease, and today's stressful situation meant that it was the worst we'd ever seen him. According to his Doctor he was very poorly indeed and if it wasn't treated properly the worst case scenario was that it could be fatal. He'd also had Colitis and really had to watch what he ate. Even though we sympathised with Gary about his condition it still wasn't out of bounds as far as our cruel humour went. We used to tell people that Gary had been involved in a traffic accident and had been knocked down by a car. This news would bring a reaction from people that would invariably be concern for Gary's welfare. After we'd grabbed their attention we then told them that the police who had arrived to investigate what had happened had found more skid marks on the bonnet of the car than on the road.

So here we were on the day of a live Television appearance and Gary was at the back of the van squatting over a Tesco carrier bag shitting and vomiting his insides out. It certainly took our minds off playing live in front of an alleged million people, but then it dawned on us that there was a distinct possibility that we wouldn't be able to play without him. We could get away with opening the show instrumentally as we had been asked to do, but there was no chance of us pulling off the other 2 songs we were scheduled to do. Panic set in and it was touch and go as to whether to send out for 4 more carrier bags! But we had free passes to use up, so we left Gary to continue his prolapsing in peace. We were situated behind the stage down a grass embankment so we were hidden from view, except that as the audience was growing people were taking positions on the top of the slope to get a better view at the side of the stage. What they didn't bargain for though was having the added bonus of watching a very ill man parking his breakfast from both ends. Gary remembers looking up to see a crowd of people with a ring (no pun intended) side seat to his predicament. So when the time came to open the show we got into position on stage with

Gary still at the back of the van. Just as we were given the 30 seconds to go countdown, he appeared on the stage, strapped on his guitar and then the 5 second countdown went to the rolling opening credits and we kicked into the song 'Two Horses'. 2 instrumental bars later we finished and the first hurdle was overcome. Gary's recovery was akin to the resurrection of Lazarus, because we thought that as the world fell out of Gary's bottom, the bottom was falling out of our world.

The other people that appeared on the show included Kerry Dixon, who was then manager of Doncaster Rovers at the time and Rotherham born comedian Duggie Brown who as well as being a regular on the '70's T.V. programme The Comedians, also had a small part in Kes, one of my favourite films. We waited for our call to get back on stage to do our main performance with Gary still filling shopping bags, and then the time came. Free To Love was the first song we performed. You couldn't really call it Country but it seemed to go down well at gigs. Looking back at the footage I am surprised how relaxed we looked with the trauma that had gone on beforehand. We played it well and there were some nice shots including one of me from the side showing my drum fill around the kit, which I knew was coming because that was a camera shot we had rehearsed during the day. I kept saying to myself "don't fuck it up, don't fuck it up!" We closed the show and as the credits rolled we managed to get through half of our second tune, 'Five String Guitar' before we faded into the ether. Time for a drink or seven I think.

My first experience in the world of television had been far more relaxed. Late one evening the telephone rang at home. It was a guy called Keith Manifold, who was a well- respected country singer-songwriter and was also an established figure on the gigging circuit both here and abroad. Gary had given him my number after Keith had asked him if he could borrow me for a project he was working on. Gary had no objection to me moonlighting, so here we were discussing the plans for a recording session. Keith explained that he'd been approached by ITV about performing the backing music to a scene in 'Peak Practice' which was a serial drama set in the Peak District. He lived in Matlock and I was living in Buxton so geography obviously played a part in our recruitment. We were booked into Nottingham's Carlton TV studios to make the backing music for the scene. So I met up with Keith and put what I had brought of my kit into his rather dilapidated Sherpa van. Once we were loaded up we set off to Nottingham down the M1. Now I find it difficult to make small talk at the best of times, so being in a van with someone who talked quite a lot put me at ease. I was quite nervous because at the time of actually travelling to the gig, I still didn't really know the song, but after a few plays on the radio cassette player (remember them?), it began to sink in. To be honest it wasn't complicated which helped.

We arrived at the studio where we met Johnny Keep (more of whom later) who was playing bass on the track, and then we were taken to the recording room to meet the engineer and he gave us a steer on what he wanted us to do. We were told to make it quite loose because we were supposed to be a 'live' band in the programme so we ran through it once and then went for the take. We went into the control room to listen and it sounded really good, but they wanted it to not sound as polished. That was the first time anyone had told me that I'd played a song too well! So we went back out to do it sloppier and it was all done in about 10 minutes flat. We packed down, said our goodbyes, and were informed that our cheques were in the post. Feeling quite pleased with myself I got back in the van and couldn't wait to get back to tell Ann all about my adventures as a TV recording artist. But wait is what I would have to do because just before Trowel Services on the M1 the fan belt decided to snap on the old Sherpa. We limped into the Services and Keith called the AA. Talk about being brought back down to earth. We waited for what seemed an eternity for the man to come. Eventually he turned up and we made our way home on the back of his tow truck with Keith apologising profusely and me saying that it didn't matter when in reality all I wanted to do was get home and relay my now not so glamorous story.

We had the episode recording of our part to look forward to a week later. This time I made my own way to the village of Crich where the scene was being shot, not wanting to run the gauntlet of another breakdown. It was a beautiful day and we had arranged to meet at the catering bus which was situated on a car park with views stretching for miles over the charming Derbyshire countryside. Crich is most famous for its tram museum and I must admit that I hadn't been there since a primary school trip. Our scene was part of episode 14 in series 6, subtitled 'Once in a Lifetime'. The storyline we were involved in was centred on the wedding of two of the doctors. The storyline was thus; the band that had originally been booked to perform at the wedding had cancelled and we were the last minute stand-ins. The joke being that they didn't realise that we were a country band and had also brought along a troop of line dancers. This didn't go down too well with the groom.

Anyway Keith, Johnny and I hung around for what seemed like hours while various TV people buzzed around with their clipboards and pens. Eventually after a cup of coffee in a specially converted London double decker bus we were told to go down to the village. Our scene was to be filmed in the village pub, so we started to set up the gear in a small corner whilst the camera crew were sorting out positions, and they put down a railroad type track for a camera to run along it. Once we had set up we waited.....and waited.... and then waited a bit more, until the main protagonists in the scene turned up. We watched a few indoor scenes and then went outside to witness a village scene with about 50 extras, which took about 6 takes. It was strange to see so many people just stood around chatting and then when given their cue, they started to mill about in exactly the same way each take. I often wondered what they talked about when they are in the background of a scene, perhaps how mind numbingly tedious it all is, and how 2 hours of standing about results in only 5 seconds of film.

We mimed our way through a take to get the camera angles, and it was handy for me to get used to not actually touching the kit whilst trying to look animated for the shot. As I was sat waiting for the actual take, Adrian Lukis, who played Doctor David Shearer in the programme came and sat next to me and began asking me questions. How long I had been playing, how difficult was it to learn to play them, and how I had got the gig on the programme. He was genuinely interested and I remember thinking at the time that he didn't have to do that, and then he asked if it was ok to have a go. I suppose this happens to all musicians irrespective of what instrument they play. This provides a major dilemma; saying no you can't and being judged as a precious wanker, or saying yes and then standing over them, wincing as they perceive that the art of playing the drums is to twat fuck out of them with all the strength they possess, which usually resembles the sound of them being thrown down a very steep set of metal stairs. I said okay, mainly because I don't regard myself as precious or indeed a wanker, plus the fact that he had shown me some recognition and courtesy. I can't remember how he performed but he still had all his teeth intact for his next scene, so presumably it went swimmingly.

So it was time for our time in the spotlight. Or in my case, a time in a very subdued light, seen through a throng of line dancing extras, stuck in a corner, under a dartboard. We did it in one take but we didn't have time to bask in the afterglow of our performance as we immediately started to pack all the instruments away so they could shoot the next series of scenes. So after a long day we headed home. I didn't bother to stop and watch the later scenes being filmed, I'd had a long day and just wanted to go back to the pub and have a beer. Tiring, thirsty work this television lark. My mum had taped it and I still have that precious piece of TV history on my shelf.

17. And In The End…

So two stints on television and awards for best band made for a good year and the gigs were getting more prestigious including playing at the annual Americana festival at Newark Showground over the next few years, starting off in one of the smaller rooms until we worked our way up to the outer main stages. But things had slowed down somewhat and cracks were starting to appear. Phill was missing more gigs which upset the balance of the band, so we'd have to draft in Gary's long serving bass player in to cover. Johnny Keep was a quietly spoken Yorkshire man with a silver tinged bushy moustache, which rested on the top of a lop-sided filthy grin. He had worked with Gary for a number of years as a duo and he was also in the Peak Practice episode with me.

Johnny was a lovely bloke and extremely laidback to the point of horizontal, and this endeared him to people, which was sometimes a good thing but other times it led to some very bizarre situations. On one occasion whilst on a duo gig with Gary, Johnny had been offered a proposal of a game of hide the sausage with a lady from the audience. Johnny was single at the time so why not? He and Gary were staying overnight so the offer to visit her caravan didn't hold out any problems. That was until he arrived there, where he found more than he had bargained for. Sat on the sofa bed, the lady's husband greeted Johnny with a cheery hello. It transpired that he was no longer able to fulfil his conjugal rights and his wife had needs that required attending to.

He was perfectly agreeable to the situation and apparently Johnny was up for the task in hand, so never one to let somebody down, he stepped up to the plate. The husband was left watching the television while they relocated to the bedroom. Without going into any biological detail he got down to work and her every needs were being attended to, so consequently everyone was contented with their situation. Time passed and things were going along very nicely when there was a knock on the bedroom door. A head appeared around the doorframe; "cup of tea Johnny?" Now if there's one thing that would most likely to cause you to 'lose' the moment, then the husband of the woman you are in the middle of shagging the arse off, offering you a brew must be up there (no pun intended) with the best. Not Johnny. After curtailing his activities for a second he looked up, and gave the guy one of his lop sided smiles. "Aye, two sugars please pal". With that he finished the job in hand, finished his brew, made his excuses and left. Legend.

Some of the best venues were the holiday camps, which normally meant better rooms, bigger crowds and not having to pack down after we'd finished playing. On the downside we sometimes had to play on the Saturday night and Sunday morning. This was the case when we were booked to play at a festival at Presthaven Sands Holiday Park in North Wales. To be fair this was one of the better seaside venues as it had been subjected to a modernisation project and was quite tastefully done out, unlike some of the other camps. We had played on the Saturday night and it was a good gig with an enthusiastic crowd, we'd sold a few cd's and posters, had our photos taken, and signed autographs, chatted to people after the show, and then had a few drinks before retiring to our caravan still buzzing from a good night. The following morning we went for breakfast and as we walked through to the large food hall, we exchanged nods and 'good morning's' with people who had been at the show and expressed some very kind compliments to us. But one incident springs to mind. We were due to give another performance on the Sunday dinnertime and had just finished sound checking when this guy approached us at the bar. He explained how he'd seen us on the Saturday night and really enjoyed the set, along with his wife and son. As we were thanking him for his kind words a young bloke walked up to us. The conversation went something like this;

Dad; "Lads, I'd like you to meet my son. I was just telling the boys in the band how much we enjoyed it last night, didn't we Graham?"

Graham; "Yeah it were good"

Us; "Thanks Graham, we really appreciate it"

Graham; "Me name's not Graham"

Stunned silence;

Us; Oh! Right, sorry about that.

Dad; "What are you talking about, of course your name's Graham"

Graham; " I've decided to change it….. to Wildcat"

More stunned silence;

Now at this particular juncture in the conversation, trying to suppress the need to laugh out loud was practically impossible. It would have also been a very cruel thing to do. All the same none of us wanted to make eye contact with each other, or speak. Eventually Graham/Wildcat broke the deadlock.

Graham/Wildcat; "When I come to festivals I always

call meself somethin' different because Graham's a boring name"

Us; "A bit like a stage name?"

Graham/Wildcat; "Yeah I suppose so"

We thanked them again and walked off back to the caravan. Afterwards I thought to myself; the world needs more Grahams/Wildcats.

We entered the new millennium as we had entered the previous couple of years by performing in Buxton. That was a symbol of the predictability of the band, plus the fact that the set had remained more or less unchanged for a long time. I was enjoying the gigs less and less, as we were playing further and further away. Then one day in late summer, whilst I was just about to go on stage at what was an important festival in Norfolk I received a telephone call from Ann telling me she had been involved in an accident with a motorbike. She was really shaken up as you would expect but I felt completely helpless because I was so far away and it was then that I thought I'd had enough and wanted to spend my weekends doing other things. I'd also missed a good friend's wedding because we had a gig and my commitment was starting to wane. Phill was thinking the same thing and we were talking about packing it in. so to keep the interest going a bit longer we embarked on recording our second album, 'Standing Out From The Crowd'. I recorded the drums in Steve's cellar using trigger pads, and Andy was getting into producing in a big way and had a little studio set up at home. It eventually saw the light of day the following year along with a website for the band. But both of us were adamant that we would see the gigs out for the rest of 2001 but that we would quit after that.

Our last gig was on Saturday 12th January 2002 at Buxton. It seemed fitting to bow out on home soil where our families could see us one last time. It was a really weird, subdued night because we knew, and the audience knew, that this was it. Once we'd finished the last encore and as soon as we were out of sight we all started crying like babies and hugging each other. It was such an intense feeling that although we'd made our minds up to leave the band, it was as if all the past years of companionship and happy memories were dying along with the demise of the group. For me it also signified my retirement from music altogether. I sold my drum kit soon after and made a clean break. Once I've made up my mind about something that's it, I just stopped playing from that day onwards.

I'd had nearly twenty years of being involved in bands and although I never managed any lasting success or fame out of it, that wasn't the point. I possibly would have handled certain situations differently given the time again, but mostly it was fun and I was lucky to be at the right age to experience one of the most creative and fast moving periods in music history. I had come from punk to Country and everything else in between.

I was brought out of retirement for one last gig. Since the mid to late nineties I had been playing in a covers band just for beer money and it gave me a release to play punk tunes again amongst other different genres. The Screaming Beefburgers consisted of my old colleagues, Alan Longden and Steve Bainbridge and was a loose and unserious set up, and although I hadn't picked up any sticks for about 18 months I was asked to play at Dave Barnett's 40th birthday bash. So here I was back in the company of three fifths of The Ruin twenty four years after we had first started out, along with a guy who'd been in it with me for most of my musical life.

It was the best gig I ever did.

18. ALL THINGS MUST PASS

Now that I have risen from my drum stool for the last time I was free to enjoy the things that I had missed out on because of previous band commitments. Firstly I was able to spend more time with my partner Ann, which meant days out shopping or visiting some of the important places in Britain that we had never been to. Really mundane stuff which seems even more so when it's written down! I had my weekends back so that also meant that I was able to finally buy a season ticket to go and watch my beloved Derby County. I had been to matches on the days when we weren't gigging but they were few and far between so I had to be content with listening to matches on the van radio, which didn't go down too well because none of the others were really into football, plus once we were out of the local area you'd lose the reception.

I was enjoying my new found freedom, and I wasn't really missing all the travelling and long days with late nights. If I was able to teleport myself from home to whichever venue we were at and just walk on stage and start playing, then after the gig I could dissolve straight back to my house, then that would suit me fine.

With no kids to hinder us we started to travel a lot more and better jobs with more money meant that I didn't miss the steady income of the band. Not that the band were earning a lot anyway, once the money had been split between the four of us there was just enough to pay for a couple of good nights out. We both decided that we weren't going to be responsible for bringing new lives into the world; Ann was training to be a teacher and pursue a career in something that she had always wanted to do, and I am only just about capable of looking after myself. There are too many unwanted babies/children in this world and we weren't going to have one just for the sake of it. We decided that we would keep rabbits instead as a way of compensation.

One life was about to leave this world however. On 23rd May 2011 my mother passed away suddenly. She felt no pain which was a comfort as well as being the complete opposite of my father. Her heart just stopped beating with no warning signs; it was typical of her not to make a fuss even in death. She would have been eighty two less than a couple of months later, a good innings as some people will tell you. There is no such thing as a good innings as far as your mother is concerned, no number is sufficient.

My father gave me the musical gene but my mother gave me my perspective; my outlook on life. She took on two jobs while I was going through school so that although we weren't spoiled, we always had a good Christmas and a summer holiday, albeit in some very strange places up and down the British Isles. Towards the end of her life her eyesight was fading and she was struggling to walk, but she was determined to not let that stop her and my brother bought her a mobility scooter so that she still had her independence.

On the anniversary of her death I place flowers at the spot where I last took her, eating fish and chips beside the canal in Whaley Bridge. If I'd have been able to hand pick my choice of parents, I couldn't have chosen anyone better than the two I was blessed with.

People still come up to me now and ask me if I am still playing the drums even though it's been many years since I packed it in. Sometimes in conversation with friends I would re-tell a story about my time as a drummer and as these got more frequent I had the idea that perhaps I should write it all down. It wasn't an ego thing, because let's face it I hardly hit the big time, just a few minor skirmishes with success here and there. Nowadays the cult of celebrity is all consuming with talent or intelligence no longer a pre-requisite. It's too easy to lament the existence of programmes such as The 'X' Factor because eventually people will tire of it as it gets more and more contrived with its 'real' stories of the contestants, and the four judges playing God with people's lives. It seems to be more about them than the actual performers. "Fame; I'm going to live forever" Well at least until week three perhaps.

I still consume a lot of music and that will carry on regardless. New bands with old music and old bands with new music, plus with the advent of social media outlets the choices are getting bigger and bigger. The need to trudge around the toilets of our towns and cities playing second fiddle to a television in the corner isn't a necessary requirement anymore. But the live music scene is now better than ever in my humble opinion, whether that's a reaction to the aforementioned televisual offerings or not, I cannot prove, but there are new venues and newer festivals catering for followers of all forms of music.

I've done my share of trudging and had some great times along the way.

Thankfully I survived to tell the tale.